Date Due

MESSAGE PREPARATION
THE NATURE OF PROOF

Erwin P. Bettinghaus

E BOBBS-MERRILL
RIES IN

Speech

Communication

Message preparation

THE NATURE OF PROOF

THE BOBBS-MERRILL SERIES IN *Speech Communication*

RUSSEL R. WINDES, *Editor*

Queens College of the City University of New York

ERWIN P. BETTINGHAUS

Michigan State University

Message

preparation

THE NATURE OF PROOF

The Bobbs-Merrill Company Inc.

A SUBSIDIARY OF HOWARD W. SAMS & CO., INC.

PUBLISHERS   INDIANAPOLIS   NEW YORK   KANSAS CITY

Editor's foreword

In persuasive communication, the advocate defends a proposition. He builds a case for his proposition through arguments that he asks his audience to believe. The persuasiveness of the advocate, the degree to which his arguments are found acceptable, often hinges on the modes of proof he elects to use. Consequently, the study of proof is extremely important to the student of communication.

Studies of proof have often been organized around two questions: What proofs are necessary to establish a proposition? What kinds of proof are necessary to persuade a given audience? The important contribution of this volume is to reunite the rhetorical and practical elements of the study of proof. Professor Bettinghaus has attempted to achieve this reunification within the context of the social sciences. Through the analytic pattern that he has established, it becomes possible to examine by the same means both the formal requirements of proof and the practical requirements of persuading a given audience.

Man has developed over the years a number of analytic frameworks for categorizing and working with arguments. These include philosophical structures, logical structures, mathematical models, and a whole series of "common-sense" methods of establishing the truth of propositions. These frameworks, however, were developed to assess rationally what was necessary to prove a proposition. None was developed to aid a communicator in predicting how an auditor would respond to an argument when it was communicated to him.

Professor Bettinghaus has made a brief report on many of the more common analytic approaches to message analysis and assesses their usefulness to the communicator in predicting the behavior of the receivers. He suggests ways in which auditors react to argumentative materials. The Toulmin Analysis is presented to help the communicator take advantage of the knowledge that we do have about human behavior.

This volume is a beginning study, not a final one. For the most part, its materials have been drawn from recent findings on behavior from speech and the social sciences. The amount of empirical evidence that we have about human behavior, however, is still extremely minute with relation to the task the communicator faces. In many places, Professor Bettinghaus has relied on information drawn from the experiences of teachers and practitioners of public address, rather than from the experiences that might be gained from careful experimentation. Care has been taken, however, to insure that "common-sense" ideas are not antithetical to the findings of current researchers. The result is a thorough and competent book, one that should prove a worthy addition to speech literature.

RUSSEL R. WINDES

Contents

vii

LIST OF FIGURES

Message preparation

THE NATURE OF PROOF

The nature of proof

Introduction

Throughout much of recorded history, man has attempted to link one set of events with another, to show that because one event happened, another also happened. He has carried the attempt into science, history, jurisprudence, and religion. Whenever someone has become convinced that he **can** establish the cause of an event, he says that he has **proved** it. This book is about **proof** and the role it plays in message preparation.

Modes of proof have changed greatly over the centuries, but the concept of proof is recognizable over a span of two thousand years. Ancient Greeks recognized confessions obtained from the torture of witnesses as valid evidence—and perfectly good proof—in their courts. A few hundred years later, the "water test" could establish the proof of a man's guilt. The accused was thrown in the water. If he swam, he was judged guilty; if he drowned, he was believed to have been not guilty. During the American colonial period, in the late 1600's, colonists accepted as proof in some courts the testimony that individuals were witches because milk turned sour after they had visited the cow barn.

Today, Americans no longer accept the water test as evidence of innocence or guilt, and most of us do not believe in witches. Nevertheless, we do remain interested in proof. We use the word in several ways, and we vary in what to accept as proof, but we realize that one of the communicator's main tasks is to supply enough evidence so that his audience will say, "That is enough. You have proved your case."

The nuclear physicist, the psychologist, the lawyer, and the policeman are all interested in proof. So are the speaker at the P.T.A. meeting, the newspaper reporter, the housewife buying soap flakes, and the man listening to a political debate. The specific needs of individuals will differ, but the concept of proof is an important consideration for many communication situations. An idea of the scope of this book can be obtained from the following series of situations hinging on an understanding of the concept of proof.

1. Perhaps the situation that is most familiar is the courtroom scene in which the attorney is defending a client against a robbery charge. The job of the prosecution is to show clearly that the defendant did commit the robbery. The defense attorney must demonstrate that the prosecution has not proved its case against the defendant. He may well tell the jury that "The prosecution has failed to prove that my client did commit this crime."

2. If one loses a sum of money, or a pocketbook, and goes to the police station or to a lost-and-found section of a store, he will be asked to "prove" that the money is his. He will be asked to show in some fashion that what was found was in fact what he lost, as well as asked to establish his right to the money or other valuables.

3. Many have observed a situation in which a number of small boys are playing. One of them declares, "I'm the toughest guy here!" It is unlikely that he will be allowed to get away with the statement without being asked to "Prove it!"

4. Every four years the United States elects a new President or retains an incumbent President. Each of the candidates presents a platform consisting of statements of what he intends to do if elected. The political campaign consists of attempts by each man to **prove** that he has the better platform, or that his qualifications will enable him to carry out his ideas more successfully than the other man. Once more, proof is important, but it seems to be a different kind of "proof" from that called for from the small boy or the loser of a twenty-dollar bill.

5. Consider the scientist. His whole professional life is involved

with proof. He may be a Charles Darwin, who came to believe that the concept of evolution was fact. To the modern scientist, however, an idea is not enough. He must also be able to **prove** to the satisfaction of his colleagues and the rest of the world that his hypotheses are correct.

6. Finally, one can look at a recent campaign supporting the fluoridation of water supplies. The proponents of fluoridation claim that taking this step will reduce the number of cavities that children are likely to have. The opponents of fluoridation say that there is no **proof** that this will happen, and they further point to possible damages to which fluoridation might be linked. Regardless of which side wins the referendum, the newspapers are likely to say after the vote is in that one side or the other "'proved their case."

Each of these situations seems to involve the **testing of ideas.** And originally, to "prove" something meant to ". . . make trial of, or to test the genuineness or qualities of . . ." a thing.[1] For the speaker, proof is still linked to testing, and although the ways in which we test ideas differ, the basic process is still the same.

Although the six situations described above seem different in many respects, some elements in each of the situations are common to the six, and common to all communication situations where proof is involved. Let us look at them again and ask just **how** the individuals involved attempted to test their ideas—to prove their case.

1. The attorney cannot take the jury back to the time at which the robbery was committed and literally show the jury that his client was not there. He is limited to trying to show through a series of statements or exhibits that his client is innocent. He may produce a witness who will swear that he saw the defendant in another town on the night of the robbery. Or he may bring in a witness to swear that the defendant could not have committed the robbery because he was playing cards with the witness at the time the crime was committed. Nevertheless, the lawyer is limited to **making statements** or to **showing exhibits** in his effort to prove that his client was innocent. He will win his case only if the jury **believes** in the witnesses he produces or is swayed by the exhibits.

2. The loser of some money might give the serial number of the bills he lost as evidence that the money belongs to him and not to

[1] **The Oxford Universal Dictionary on Historical Principles**, 3rd ed. (Oxford: Clarendon Press, 1955), p. 1607.

someone else. For most of us this would be very strong evidence, and we might well believe the individual's story. Or the loser might describe in detail where he lost the money. If he states accurately where the money was lost and found, we might believe his story and turn the money over to him.

3. The small boy who wants to prove that he is the toughest boy on the block has several alternatives. He may make a series of statements on how high he can jump, how fast he can run, or how far he can throw a football. He may offer to let the other boys feel his muscles. Or he may offer to fight any of the other boys. In any of these instances, the boy either makes statements or demonstrates his abilities until the others decide to believe him.

4. The Presidential candidate cannot ask the electorate to feel his muscles—at least not literally. The candidate is confined to words. He must make statements about his past actions, his present intentions, and his future expectations, in the hope that the voters will eventually come to believe in him and in the party he represents.

5. The scientist must also depend on the beliefs of other people in his ideas and hypotheses. He may make a series of statements, in order to show that his hypothesis is correct; or he may offer a series of demonstrations. He may show his listeners a series of fossils and then claim that these exhibit a particular relationship to present-day animals. The great anthropologist, L. S. B. Leakey, produced a number of fossil remains from Africa that he claimed were very distant relations of present-day mankind. The average viewer looking at Professor Leakey's exhibits might easily conclude that they all look very much alike. He cannot interpret the exhibits himself, yet he might decide to believe in Leakey's hypotheses because he respects Professor Leakey.

6. The case of the fluoridation campaign is probably most representative of the role that proof plays in message preparation. Both sides appeal to the electorate to accept the position that they represent through speeches, news stories, and advertisements. Both sides are limited in their efforts by the amount of material available and the time that they have. They must prepare their communications in such a way that listeners will want to accept their statements as proof of their position. They can present statistics showing that fluoridation results in thirty-five per cent fewer cavities after ten years of use. They can show pictures of teeth which have turned

black from the application of too much fluoride. They can appeal to religious beliefs against adding medicines to water supplies. They can appeal to economic beliefs and point to the saving on dentist bills. But both sides are limited to what they can present in their speeches and in their stories. What they must obtain is **belief** in their side of the question on the part of the electorate.

The concept of belief shows up in each situation discussed. When the belief of listeners is obtained, the communicator has proved his case. This is the goal of all persuasion and the reason for attempting such a difficult thing as proof. Belief is of such importance that Chapter 2 will be devoted to a discussion of belief and oral communication.

A second common element is the means by which proof can be obtained. The individual who wishes to prove his case and secure belief in his ideas can do so only by producing **evidence** to support his ideas. That is, he must make statements relating to the case or provide a demonstration that supports his case. He must have some kind of **evidence,** and it must be related in some way to the proposition in which he wishes to secure belief. The nature and types of evidence are discussed fully in Chapter 4.

The common elements in these six situations suggest a definition of proof: **Proof is the process of using evidence to secure belief in an idea or statement.**

This definition forms the basis for the remainder of this book. It will be used to examine the various parts of the definition and expand on them with two goals: the reader should learn to use evidence to secure belief in his ideas. He should learn to listen to evidence being presented by another in such a way as to be able to test the adequacy of the material as support for the other's ideas.

Speech communication and communicator intent

The nuclear physicist, the psychologist, and the policeman are concerned with proof in situations that do not necessarily involve oral communication. The discussion in this volume, however, will be limited to situations involving speech communication. This limitation is not at all an inhibiting one. Most of our ideas, memories, beliefs, and knowledge have been gained through communication; and the greatest part of our communication activity is through speech communication, through talking and listening to others.

Many students of speech communication argue that all communication has a persuasive nature. The author tends to agree with the type of analysis that stresses the necessity for attitude change even when the intent of the communicator is to have the individual learn a series of facts. But although one agrees with this general analysis, it seems useful to look specifically at the relation of proof to the intentions of the communicator.

In many cases the speaker has the primary intention of producing learning on the part of the listener or listeners. If one were to ask the speaker what he wanted the listener to be able to do after his speech is over, he might suggest that he wanted the listener to repeat some of the speech materials or to perform a task described in the speech. In such a case, one would say that the speaker's primary intention was **to inform.** In other types of speeches, the communicator might have the primary task of modifying an auditor's attitude. He might not care whether the listener repeated parts of the speech or recognized the speech if he heard it again, but he does want the listener to become either more or less favorable toward the topic under discussion. In this case, one would say that the primary intention of the speaker was **to persuade.** And in still a third type of situation, a number of speakers may be engaged in persuasive speaking, but deliberately representing different attitudinal positions. This is called debate, and it is really a special case of persuasion. It is a special case in that the intent of the various speakers is to persuade, but to do so while observing certain rules of conduct regarding the handling of evidence.

If one looks at the role of evidence in oral communication, he sees that the intention of the speaker determines the way in which he uses evidence. At first glance, it may seem that informative speaking consists merely of a recital of statements of fact—of pieces of evidence. Indeed, a popular expression has been derived from the speaker who says, "I'll just give them the facts; plain, simple facts." This is, of course, oversimplification. People do not necessarily learn "plain, simple" facts. They have to be led from simple kinds of statements to the complex ones in which the communicator is more interested. Most of us would consider it a fact that the earth was round. But imagine attempting to tell a savage who believed that the world was flat that he was wrong. In order to be sure that the savage had "learned," one would have to present many small bits of evidence. Only in this way could he be sure that the savage could finally understand his position. Only then he could assume that his listener had actually learned the materials of interest. This same kind of analysis of the learning process and its relation to proof is necessary for the kind of learning situation in which one wishes the individual to be able to perform some task at the conclusion of the speech. If the objective is to teach him to thread a moving-picture projector, it must be accomplished through the presentation of small bits of material, taking him step by step through the process. The presentation of material in informative speaking is not merely the presentation of simple facts. The listener must be led to feel that he has a reason for learning.

Similar needs for evidence exist in the situation in which the communicator wishes the listener to form or change an attitude toward some idea. It is possible to make a speech in which there is not one statement of fact, not one single piece of evidence. But it is extremely difficult to do so. Even the most emotional, biased speaker has some evidence in his speech.

An example of the importance of evidence in changing attitudes can be observed in considering the alternatives open to a speaker supporting a school-bond campaign. He can operate completely in the area of opinions and say: "We need more money for schools. This is a good proposal. Our children deserve the best, and this bond campaign will give it to them." Here, a communicator attempts persuasion through a series of statements that are not factual, but judgmental or inferential. Probably, it would be more persuasive for him to say:

> Last week our schools were visited by the State Department of Education. Officials from that department report that we will lose our state accreditation if we do not provide more classrooms and more teachers for our basic courses. If we lose our state accreditation, our children cannot be accepted at the state university. In order for them to have the same advantages as the children of other school systems, it is necessary for us to pass the proposed bond issue.

Which is the better approach? Most of us would probably say that a more persuasive approach has been used in the second example, where evidence and reasoning are employed to draw a conclusion designed to change a listener's mind. Evidence cannot be ruled out of persuasive speaking. Proof is just as important when the intention is to persuade as it is when one is attempting to get a listener to learn a series of statements of fact.

Finally, consider the special case of debate. It has already been emphasized that debates are persuasive situations in which individuals representing more than one point of view are all communicating in the hope of convincing the audience that their point of view is the more correct one. Evidence plays a doubly important role in this situation. Possibly, when only one speaker is advocating a particular position, the listener will need a minimum of facts, of substantive proof, before he is willing to agree with the speaker. But when several speakers are present and different points of view are represented, he will not agree so easily. The nature of the evidence presented by different speakers is an important factor in determining the winner of the debate. There are, of course, many other important factors. The speaker with the better delivery will have an advantage; so will the speaker with the best-known reputation, the speaker with the best choice of words, and the speaker who has marshalled the most acceptable set of evidence for his position, or who can support his position with the clearest reasoning.

In some situations, delivery is undoubtedly the determining fact in an individual's decision to accept the conclusions presented by one side in a debate. In others, the reputation of the speaker, or his choice of words, may be decisive. In many, many others, the decision may be made on the basis of the evidence presented. Whether the debate is in a courtroom, where materials are presented according to an elaborate set of rules, or in a Parent-Teachers meeting debating the merits of compulsory gymnastics for high-school students, the communicator who can bring a better set of evidence to bear on his topic has an advantage.

Most of us tend to look at evidence as useful only in a courtroom. Television drama and newspaper coverage certainly support that tendency. But evidence is important in all speaking situations. Whether one is sitting across the table from a friend or group of friends, or speaking from the public platform, he needs evidence to secure the attention of auditors, to interest them in learning the material he presents, and to get them to accept his proposals.

Certainly, one cannot argue that the mere presentation of various kinds of evidence will necessarily result in effective communication.

But unless a speaker knows how to use evidence appropriately, his possession of other communication skills will not make for effective communication either.

Material evidence and our language system

Up to now, an assumption has been implicit in this discussion, the assumption that evidence is concerned only with facts, that only statements of fact can be used as evidence. Such a view is too narrow.

There are several methods of talking about language, of categorizing the sentences we use. The linguist, for example, might like to classify sentences according to the ways in which the nouns and verbs within the sentence are arranged. This kind of classification, however, would be of little help in studying evidence. A better method might be to look at the intention of the communicator as a basis for a classification system of the kinds of sentences likely to be used as evidence.

The sentence that is intended to inform the listener about something in the physical world is called a **statement of fact,** a **report,** or an **observation.** Statements of fact form the basis for all evidence, whether the statement of fact is given directly as evidence, or has been used to arrive at some other statement. Examples of statements of fact that might be used as evidence by a communicator include: "There are eleven fish in that tank." "The nation spent five billion dollars last year on space flight." "There has never been a case of tuberculosis in our city." "World War II started in September 1939." "The paper reports that there were three people killed in auto accidents last year." "An airplane lands at O'Hare Field in Chicago every minute." These statements have a characteristic that distinguishes them from all other kinds of sentences. They can be **verified.** Statements of fact are sentences that can be labeled as either true or false. If one counts the number of fish in the tank and finds that there are not eleven fish but fourteen, he would label as false the sentence "There are eleven fish in that tank." Note that we do not say that this is **not** a statement of fact. It is. But it is a false statement of fact. **Verification is a word describing the process we go through to determine whether or not a sentence is a true statement of fact or a false statement of fact.**

Since many of the kinds of evidence discussed in this book will be composed of statements of fact, it will be useful to look a bit more closely at the process of verification.

There are two ways in which statements of fact may ordinarily be verified. The truth of the statement may be checked by going from the statement to the real world and making an actual check. If someone tells us that there are three traffic lights at a particular intersection, we can go to the intersection and count them. If we find three lights we say that the individual had made an accurate report. If we read that nine thousand high-school seniors have applied for college scholarships at a particular university, we could go to the registrar at that university, ask him for the file of scholarship applications, and proceed to count them. The results of our counting will determine whether this is an accurate statement or not.

If one had to verify literally all the statements of fact to which he is exposed every day, most of his time would be spent in the process of verification. Moreover, many statements of fact are either difficult or almost impossible, to verify. The average individual cannot verify the sentence: "The tallest tree in the world is 372 feet high." Most of us, therefore, have to rely on verifications provided by other individuals. Everyone relies on the verifications of others to a surprising degree. Almost all statements of fact that one reads in the daily newspaper are believed or at least accepted without personal verifications. One reads textbooks on history, science, art, and chemistry and seldom bothers to check the accuracy of their observations.

When an individual takes a statement of fact made by someone else as true, and does not verify the statement himself, he places trust in the reputation of the other communicator not to make statements that are false. In such a situation, if one cannot personally verify the statement he employs a second method of verification: he checks the reputation of the communicator making the statement of fact. Chapter 4 will look at methods of checking statements that cannot be personally verified.

In many of the most interesting communication situations, statements of fact are not used directly. Rather, reports and observations have been used to make another type of sentence that we call an **inferential statement.** Some examples of inferences are: "The man was afraid." "Red China wants to start a Third World War." "The girl doesn't like the boy." "Our children are getting an inferior education." "The Governor doesn't want to give the University enough money." All these statements are inferential. They are based on a statement of fact, or on a series of observations, but they are **not** factual statements themselves.

Consider the sentence "The man was afraid." This statement might be made on the basis of observing that the man was sweating, or had turned pale, or had run away. After making the observation, the observer makes the inference. Or take the statement "The man had a poor attitude toward his job." Again, this sentence may have been generated from observations that the man was late to work, that he took overly long coffee breaks, that he left early, or that his work was not so good as that done by others. Again, the statement "The man had a poor attitude toward his job" was made on the basis of a series of factual statements, but it is not a statement of fact in itself. Note that one could be wrong in making both inferential statements. He might just as well have concluded that "The man was sick," as that "The man was afraid." And in the second case, he might have concluded that "The man had not received proper training on the job," rather than that "The man had a poor attitude toward his job."

Inferential statements are important in any consideration of the concept of proof. In many sciences and arts, inferences form the basic materials with which one must work. Any inferential statement is a statement made about something that cannot be known directly on the basis of information available. Thus one must make inferences when he wants to find out what Indian tribes inhabited the United States one thousand years ago. He needs inferences when he wants to find out who committed a particular crime, when he attempts to make medical diagnoses, or when he wishes to make statements about the intentions of the Soviet Union toward the United States.

In the detailed examination of kinds of evidence in the second part of this book, inferential statements are shown to serve as a basic form of evidence. But this beginning analysis should alert the reader to the two major dangers of the inferential statement: the first has already been mentioned, i.e., the inference may be incorrectly drawn from the statements of fact on which it is based. Later, several models will be suggested to help the communicator in drawing inferences correctly. The second danger is that one may fail to recognize an inference when it is made and may operate as if the statement were a statement of fact. Again, a set of rules will be suggested to help in distinguishing inferential statements from factual statements.

The third type of sentence that must be distinguished in considering material evidence is the **judgmental statement.** Judgmental statements do not have a primary relationship to the physical world. Judgments include such sentences as: "San Francisco is a beautiful city." "That football team is the best in the state." "That legislator is prejudiced against my company." "This book ought to be banned from our libraries." All these are judgments. They do not say much about the real world, and they cannot be verified. But they say something about the individual making the statement. Judgmental statements indicate the kind of values or attitudes the maker of the statement holds, but they do not tell anything about the nature of the physical world, **unless** one knows something about the man making the statement. Only when something is known about the bases for a judgmental statement can it be used as evidence.

One means of distinguishing the judgment from the inferential statement or the factual statement is to look at the kinds of words in the sentence. Words such as "beautiful," "artistic," "wonderful," "horrible," or "happy" are the kinds of words that one finds in a judgment. They are words whose meaning will differ depending on to whom the listener is listening. It is certainly true that even words that we think we know the meaning of may give us trouble, but words that clearly express approval or disapproval of what we are talking about identify the statement as a judgment.

Judgmental statements are tempting. They allow one to place values easily on ideas, objects, and people. And when engaged in persuasion, the temptation to make a judgment serve instead of a series of factual statements is high. It will be shown that judgments are used as material evidence, but that their use is limited.

Summary

This chapter has defined proof as the process of using evidence to secure belief in an idea or statement. It has suggested that the communicator may be engaged in communication in order to inform his listeners, or to persuade them, or he may be engaged in the special situation we call argumentation. In each of these situations, the communicator is concerned with proof and with the materials of proof we refer to as evidence. And finally, it has examined the kinds of sentences with which the communicator will be concerned when he selects materials to use in proving his case. Factual statements, inferential statements, and judgmental statements, representing different intentions on the part of the communicator, can be seen as a different view of reality. All have to be kept in mind when looking at the concept of proof in detail.

TWO

The nature of belief

The need to study the concept of belief

In the first chapter, proof was defined as the process of using evidence to secure belief in ideas. Later chapters will be devoted to an examination of various types of evidence and the ways in which evidence can be used in constructing speech materials. Before making that examination, however, it will be helpful to look at the concept of **belief,** the goal of all communication.

The first volume of this series noted that all speech communication results in persuasion, in changes in the attitudes and beliefs of auditors. The fact that a speaker intends only to provide information for his audience, or intends only to entertain his audience, may obscure the fact that persuasion will occur along with learning or entertainment. Understanding persuasion means understanding **belief,** and when we say that persuasion has taken place, we are saying that we have changed or modified some individual's belief.

An auditor's beliefs help determine what he listens to, and to whom he is willing to listen. An auditor already favorable toward the position we are advocating is far more willing to listen to us and to believe what we say. An entertainer can engage the attention of

14

an audience only if his auditors have enough belief in his potential as a humorist to be willing to hear him out. Thus in a very real sense, belief lies at the base of all attempts at communication. The speech communicator must understand the bases for belief.

This understanding is important for two reasons. First, the speaker must understand the concept of belief in order to phrase his message. That is, he must know what beliefs he is interested in changing or establishing in his listeners. No matter whether his overt intent is persuasion or learning, the speaker must be concerned with an examination of beliefs in order to achieve his goal. When the goal is learning, i.e., when the speaker is interested in the retention of his material, the extent of the listener's belief in that material may determine the listener's willingness to expose himself to the material. If a student does not feel that mathematics will ever be of any help to him, it is not likely that he will be interested in listening to a lecture on mathematics; and if forced to listen, he may learn little from the lecture. When the aim of the speaker is to secure some change in overt behavior on the part of the audience, e.g., to obtain a vote for a candidate, he will at least have to secure the belief of the audience in that candidate and what he stands for before the behavior change will occur. Attitude change clearly concerns the speaker's ability to facilitate a change in belief on the part of the audience.

The second reason for the importance of an understanding of belief is not so easy to see: the speaker must be able to **use belief to secure belief.** He may want the listener to become favorably disposed toward a particular piece of legislation. If he knows that the listener already favors a consequence of that legislation, he may use the belief in the consequence to secure belief in the legislation. For example, many people are currently worried about the world's population explosion. They believe that the population must soon level off or the world will have serious problems in sustaining present living standards. The speaker who wishes to elicit support for a measure allowing the United States to give assistance to foreign governments in developing birth-control practices might well use his listener's concern about the rising population to support his contentions about birth control. An advertising manager may have to secure belief in the effectiveness of a particular make of automobile. If he knows that the listener believes that engine performance is the most important attribute of any car, he might word an advertisement something like this:

> An automobile ought to run well. In city driving, or on the open highway, any car must perform consistently. That is why we start designing cars from the inside out. The best automotive engineers in the country have paid attention to the design of the engine and transmission system of this car.

What the advertiser has done here is to make use of a previously held belief to influence belief in a related proposition. He has used one belief to secure belief in another proposition.

Let us examine a few communication situations where belief plays an important part in determining the speaker's success.

1. Recent years have seen the re-emergence of Africa as an area of major world concern. The United States has sent Peace Corps representatives to assist the emerging African states in developing their education, health, and economic systems. The main tool the Peace Corps representative has is his ability to **talk** a villager into trying a new idea. But the belief systems of many Africans are quite different from those of the Peace Corpsman. In spite of intense efforts by Christian missionaries and a thousand years of Moslem proselytizing, basic African belief patterns in magic, witchcraft, and ritual still prevail in many areas. The tribesman may not know that disease is caused by germs or viruses. He is more likely to believe that his illness is caused by magic and will blame his misfortunes on a witch doctor presumably hired by his enemies. The Westerner may believe that his job will be easy. He draws a sample of blood (from his own arm, because the native will not let his own blood be drawn for fear that it will be used in witchcraft against him) and shows the native that there are "little animals" in his blood that are causing him to feel bad. Simple? The task is not this easy. Basic belief patterns are not so easily changed. The native's reply might well be, "What witch doctor placed the little animals in your blood?" He might even offer (if he liked the Westerner) to tell him whom to hire to get the little animals out of his blood.

2. Every year, shortly after the Thanksgiving holiday has passed, small children all over the United States begin to talk about Santa Claus. Their belief in the toy-giving potential of the little fat man

has amazed and delighted generations of parents. During this annual period, compliance with parental requests is at an all-time high, a large portion of it probably as a result of a belief in Santa Claus. But shortly after Christmas, appeals to Santa Claus have little or no effect on the behavior of the same small children. When the child reaches school age, moreover, he usually becomes quite suspicious about the good Saint's existence. This belief is certainly related to behavior, but it seems to be quite different from the African's belief in witchcraft. If the belief is not a dominant part of the individual's personality, it disappears at an early age.

3. In several areas of the United States, small religious sects believe in extremely literal interpretations of the Bible. Their interpretations extend to their analyses of the physical world around them solely in terms of words used in the Bible to explain physical phenomena. Several years ago, newspapers in the United States printed a story about the minister in a small Southern town who told his congregation that the sky was located forty miles above the earth and that it consisted of a covering separating Heaven from earth. For this minister, the stars were holes in the covering, and he firmly maintained that when we would finally be able to reach the sky, we would find Heaven on the other side of the covering. When reporters talked to him about evidence obtained from modern science, he refused to listen, saying only, "You will see that I am right when we are able to fly that high." One wonders what has happened to his beliefs since astronauts have ridden space capsules far above his sky. But the beliefs of the listener helped determine what he listened to and what he accepted as proof.

4. In spite of the intentions of peace and friendship declared by the Western and Soviet worlds, the basic belief patterns of peoples on either side of the Iron Curtain differ. The differences may not be so great as some would maintain, but they are great enough to cause widespread suspicion and mistrust. An announcement by the Soviet Union that their military expenditures will be cut will probably be greeted in the United States by an official statement that the Soviets merely want to lull us into a false sense of security. A similar announcement by the United States will in all probability be greeted by Moscow with a statement that the Americans are doing this only because they wish the Soviets to lay themselves open to attack. In both cases, basic belief patterns and

structures lead individuals to look at similar evidence in different ways. If these belief structures are very different, evidence convincing to one country is not likely to be convincing to the other country, and vice versa. The communicator who wishes to be successful in talking to either side will have to examine closely the structure and content of the beliefs held by Russians or Americans. Beliefs are, again, an important element in determining the success of the speaker.

In the four sample situations, beliefs differ in content and in kind. The differences in the situations are also important in determining the ways in which communication will be initiated and received. Many other variables could be mentioned to point up the importance of beliefs. The layman typically accepts and believes evidence that the trained lawyer might not accept. The college-educated person is likely to have a different set of beliefs from those of the person who has only a grade-school education. People from one religious background look at the world differently than do individuals from a different religious background. Children will hold some beliefs in common with their parents but will also have beliefs that differ from those of their parents and grandparents. Women have beliefs that differ from those of men. Indeed, every individual differs from every other individual in the nature and content of his belief system.

The definition of belief

Everyone has at least some meaning for the term **belief.** But a fuller discussion of the concept will enable us to use it more precisely. The term seems to be used in several ways. People talk about "believing in the Democratic party," or "believing in science," or "believing in President Johnson." They also use the term to refer to the truth of a proposition or statement. People say "I believe that we should have compulsory arbitration of labor disputes," or "I believe that all Americans should be allowed to vote," or "I believe that this movie is the best one I have seen this year."

First, the term belief seems to be used in referring to an individual's **placing trust or confidence in a person or thing.** During the depression of the 1930's, many Americans placed their trust in the abilities of President Franklin D. Roosevelt. In the 1960's, many

Negro citizens have placed their belief in the Reverend Martin Luther King. They **believe** in him and are inclined to believe in the truth of any statements he might make. They do not think that Dr. King is "true," but merely that he can be trusted, and that the statements he makes can be believed.

Second, to say that one believes in a person or in a concept seems to be different from **accepting a proposition as true.** All of us tend to accept or reject the statements we hear or read—whether about dating, animals, movies, food, or television. We make or hear statements about politics, religion, history, science, and the future; and we say that we may either **believe** or **disbelieve** in these statements.

A careful look at these two ways of describing beliefs discloses that although they appear to be different, they have much in common. To say that someone believes in a person is to say that he accepts a set of statements about the person as either true or false. For example, to say that a person "believes in President Johnson" is to say that the person feels that statements about President Johnson's competence, trustworthiness, ability, and goodness are true. Looked at in this way, the basic definition of belief must be in terms of **accepting a proposition or statement as true.** This definition is an important one for the speaker to understand.

If a speaker is going to analyze an audience by looking at the beliefs that its members hold, our definition suggests that he find out what statements they would accept as true. If he wishes to change the behavior or attitude of audience members, he must first find out what beliefs they currently hold and then be able to state the ways in which the proposed speech material differs from these current beliefs. If one is going to write a speech, the statements used in the speech will be related to the beliefs he holds, and one of his objectives is to make sure that the statements will also be related to the beliefs the audience holds. In each situation, the speaker must be aware of the statements he accepts as true, as well as those of the audience that he is addressing.

Description of beliefs

Besides defining the concept of belief, the speaker must also find some way of describing specific beliefs. Almost every statement an individual makes has at least some relation to a belief he holds, and it is not very useful to talk about beliefs in terms of the thousands of specific statements that might be made. The speaker must be able to set up a system that will categorize statements systematically.

Beliefs can be described in terms of the content of the statement. We can talk about statements that are made about the population explosion, poverty, war, peace, education, and so forth. Each topic or content area may have many statements made about it; for example, the communicator may say that "The population problem is more serious in India than in the United States," or that "The population problem is bad and getting worse." These are two different statements made about the same content area.

A second way of describing beliefs is in terms of the intensity with which they are held. Everyone has some beliefs that he seldom changes and about which he feels very strongly. He may believe very strongly that the Republican party is the only political party presenting a useful platform. He may believe very strongly that the United States has the best form of government in the world today. He may be very strongly against any increases in the income tax. But everyone also has a number of beliefs that he feels less strongly about and that he might be willing to change. He might feel that the school his son goes to needs a new baseball diamond, but he does not really care much one way or the other. Or he may prefer one brand of beer but be quite willing to drink any other brand that is offered. Some beliefs are held very intensely, whereas other beliefs are held much less intensely.

Thus a more accurate description of beliefs would describe them in terms of the intensity with which they are held, and in terms of the specific content of the belief. To measure the beliefs an individual holds, first ascertain how interested he is in the general content area. For example, ask the individual whether he is interested in the topic "the population explosion." Ask whether he finds messages about the topic to be "interesting" or "uninteresting." To find out what his beliefs are toward a specific statement from the general content area, ask whether he "favors legislation to control the population explosion." One could get a more precise answer from the respondent by asking him if he is "strongly in favor," "moderately in favor," "neutral toward," "moderately against," or "strongly against" such legislation.

The method suggested is one frequently used by the behavioral scientist to find out what beliefs and attitudes an individual holds. The speaker will find it useful to go one step further. It is helpful to know how an individual regards the major topic of one's speech. But it would be even more helpful to know how he feels about related topics. If an individual says that he is in favor of legislation to help control the population explosion, the speaker might also like to ask how the listener feels about birth control, job training, government food programs, emigration, and other topics that are related to the population problem. In other words, the speaker attempts to build up a picture of the auditor's entire **belief structure.** Doing so, however, is easier to write about than to accomplish. For most speaking situations, the speaker will not be able to ask the listeners what their beliefs are. He will be forced to make his analysis on the basis of predictions of what people probably will believe, given the characteristics that he can discover about the audience.

It is easier to find methods of estimating what the beliefs of a particular group of people are or are not if one realizes that beliefs are not held randomly. Each individual builds up a **system** or structure of beliefs that is, in part, unique to him. But his beliefs will tend to be internally consistent. We do not expect an individual to believe both that democracy is the hope of the world, and also that the United States should become a Communist state. We do not expect him to believe strongly in the separation of Church and State, and also believe that the government should sponsor prayers in the public schools. These would be inconsistent beliefs, and ordinarily we do not hold beliefs that are inconsistent with one another.

Statements about consistency have to be qualified. Certainly, at times an individual apparently holds two beliefs that seem inconsistent. After careful examination, however, we usually find that he himself has found some way to reconcile the conflicting beliefs. Many people believe that smoking is related to lung cancer, yet they continue to smoke. If asked to explain this apparent inconsistency, they might suggest that to stop smoking makes them eat more, and that overweight leads to high blood pressure and an increased chance of heart trouble. Another example might be the individual who states frequently that a particular brand of automobile is the best one on the market. If we see him driving a new car of a different make, we might be tempted to ask him about the inconsistencies of his position. He may not see any inconsistency at all. His position may be that he does feel that the other car is better, but that he "got a better deal" on this one than on his preferred choice. Or he may claim that his wife really made the choice of the car he is driving. People use many ways to explain the beliefs they hold and the behaviors they exhibit. The one thing that is sure is that they will try to use explanations that "make sense" to them, although they may not make sense to anyone else.

Individuals hold a series of beliefs and hold them with varying degrees of intensity. But individuals also have a series of **disbeliefs,** and these, too, are organized into systems. Milton Rokeach, a psychologist who has written extensively about belief systems, suggests that individuals may have entire series of belief-disbelief systems:

> The reader may note our use of the term **belief-disbelief system,** and possibly object that it sounds somewhat academic. Is not the disbelief system merely the mirror-image of the belief system, and thus unnecessary? Our own observations lead us to propose that this may not be the case. We will put forward the idea that every system is asymmetrical rather than symmetrical; it includes on the one hand a system of beliefs that one accepts, and on the other, a **series** of systems that one rejects.[1]

An individual may **believe** in the supremacy of democracy, the necessity for birth control, the freedom of speech, the usefulness of Salk vaccine, and the power of the New York Yankees. He may **disbelieve** in equality for Negroes, the utility of divorce, drinking regulations for college students, and foreign aid. Disbelief is not a passive concept and it is not merely the inversion of a belief. An individual may believe strongly in the necessity for birth control, but this does not mean that he will necessarily disbelieve in large families. He may disbelieve in foreign aid, but this does not mean that he believes in refusing to help foreign countries. The concepts an individual believes in may have no seeming relationship to those he disbelieves in, and we are forced to discuss both the belief and disbelief systems of an individual.

Talking about the presence of belief systems is not enough. The communicator must be able to make some attempt at describing

[1]Milton Rokeach, **The Open and Closed Mind: Investigations into the Nature of Belief Systems and Personality Systems** (New York: Basic Books, 1960), p. 32.

those systems, in such a way that knowledge of the belief systems will be helpful to him in constructing his message. Rokeach suggests that each belief system has at least three layers. He conceives of the belief system as organized along a central-peripheral dimension. One set of beliefs is **central,** i.e., composed of beliefs that can be called "primitive" beliefs. These may be beliefs that the person has about the world around him, about religion, about the kinds of people the world contains, and perhaps most important, about his own self concept. These beliefs and disbeliefs can be characterized as intensely held and as difficult for the communicator to change. They can, however, be used as material to change less important beliefs.

The second level of belief is what Rokeach calls the **intermediate** region. This part of the belief-disbelief structure is concerned with an individual's beliefs about authorities. No one can hope to get all the information he needs to live and operate in the world from his own observations alone. He must depend on the opinions and reports of others. But which authority is chosen for an individual is a matter of belief, rather firmly held belief. Thus one person may believe firmly that if it "appears in the **Times,** it can be believed," whereas another believes that only television can give accurate news. One man may believe that only the President is really equipped to give the public the "facts," whereas another will believe that the government never tells a straight story. The beliefs and disbeliefs held about authority are important for the speaker to assess in writing a message, because if he cites an authority that is disbelieved by his audience, the entire message is likely to be disbelieved.

The final level of the belief-disbelief structure is the **peripheral** region. Rokeach defines the peripheral level as containing those specific beliefs that are derived from central or intermediate beliefs. An example of a peripheral belief is the statement "I believe that the United States should expand its foreign-aid program." Here is a specific belief that is linked to some intermediate and central beliefs. The individual may come to the peripheral belief because he heard someone he respects make statements about the importance of foreign aid. He may believe very strongly in the "brotherhood of man" or in "helping your neighbor." If the speech communicator knows something about the intermediate and central beliefs of an individual, he can make predictions regarding the nature of that person's peripheral beliefs.

In describing beliefs, the communicator can assess the specific nature of the belief, in terms of the content area to which it refers. He can also make some assessment of the intensity with which it is held. And finally, he can describe the belief in terms of a belief-disbelief structure, and perhaps assign the belief under question to a central, intermediate, or peripheral region.

Prediction of beliefs

The reader who is interested in proving his case, or in constructing a speech designed to persuade an audience, may well complain at this point that he thinks this discussion interesting, but that he needs help in finding out what the beliefs of his audience are. After all, it has been indicated that people hold varied and complex belief structures. Moreover, when one is sitting in a study attempting to compose a speech, it is difficult to make predictions about the audience that he will be facing. Indeed, the complexity of people would seem to point to the impossibility of ever finding out, in anything more than the most superficial fashion, what any group believes. Let us point out that the communicator will probably never be able to detail completely what beliefs his audience holds. But one may say that predictions can be made about the belief-disbelief systems of an audience that will be more helpful in constructing the message to be delivered than operating without any knowledge of the audience at all.

The first point is easy to understand. The communicator usually faces an audience composed of individuals whom he has met only casually or not at all. He may have only general information about the audience. For example, a communicator who is delivering a speech to an audience interested in Peace Corps training might know that the members of the audience were drawn from a university community, and that they were interested in the Peace Corps; but he probably knows no more than that. In another case, a speaker might be addressing a group interested in hospital care. The group might be drawn from all over the community, and, except for their presumed interest in the functions of the hospital, he might know nothing directly about the opinions, attitudes, and information level of its members. In either of these situations, the speaker could never expect to detail completely the belief-disbelief structure of the members of the audience.

Although communicators can never hope to make a complete analysis of their audience, they should at least attempt to make **some** predictions of the beliefs that a particular audience is likely to hold. The speaker can attempt to infer what kinds of beliefs are held by his auditors from those characteristics he is able to find out about them. For example, let us suppose that the communicator is speaking to a P.T.A. group at a local school, anywhere in the United States. He has available to him a tremendous amount of information about the general nature of his audience. He knows that the upper limit of age represented is not likely to be more than fifty and the lower limit might be twenty-five. He knows that his listeners are going to be interested in and have beliefs about children. He can guess that there are likely to be more women than men present, because more women attend P.T.A. meetings than do men. He knows that this group is likely to represent the so-called middle-class population of the United States, because schools for children of the very wealthy and of the very poor are somewhat less likely to have organized P.T.A. groups that plan programs with speakers. If he knows the city and the locality within the city, a two-minute drive in areas around the school may tell him that this is probably a suburban group, or perhaps a group of factory employees. Talking to the chairman or chairwoman for just a few minutes before the program starts may help the speaker avoid certain errors. He might thus find out that this group in general comes from a particular nationality background, or that they all have common occupational backgrounds.

Once the speaker has information about the group, he must find some way of using that information to predict the kinds of beliefs or disbeliefs the audience might have. For example, a group having children is likely to be sensitive to and have specific beliefs about new health treatments for children's diseases. A group of factory employees may be expected to have favorable beliefs regarding labor unions in the United States. A group of young suburban couples would be unlikely to have strong, positive beliefs in the values of Medicare financed through additional social security taxes. These are all **inferences,** inferences made about the beliefs that people hold from data that can be gathered without asking a single question about an individual's beliefs. As in dealing with all such inferences, the communicator could be wrong in attempting to predict what a particular belief might be from other characteristics, but making the attempt is usually better than not taking beliefs into account at all.

There are many characteristics that indicate the beliefs we hold. In particular, the kinds of groups we belong to may help determine our specific beliefs. People who have children are more likely to favor increased support for public schools in the community than will people who do not have children. Thus this group membership, i.e., having children, becomes a predictor of certain attitudes. Some of the characteristics or groups that a communicator can usually obtain specific information on include:

1. The interests of individuals change with the **age** of the individual. Speaking to a teen-age audience is certainly different from speaking to an audience of young married people or of retired couples. The average age of our audience tells a great deal about the kinds of beliefs they are likely to have, as well as the interests, attitudes, and opinions they might be expected to express. One might object to this generalization by saying that after all, most audiences are spread across many different ages, and that age is not a very good predictor. Experience tells us that this spread of age seldom happens. Most audiences will have a fairly narrow range of ages or will be composed of two different age ranges. One is likely to be talking to children, teen-agers, young married couples, older married groups, and so on until he reaches groups of individuals in the "Golden Years." Or he will face audiences that are mixed across two or more age groups, such as fathers and sons, or women's groups in two age ranges. But it is seldom that the noncelebrated speaker faces audiences composed of an even mixture of people from all age ranges.

2. Many of the activities that people engage in, with which speakers are concerned, happen in groups of men or women only. Women brought together for a garden-club meeting can be expected to have a different set of expectations from those of a group of men brought together for a speech on conservation practices. Most of us

would agree that men and women may hold similar sets of beliefs, but when men and women are operating in different social groupings, the beliefs that are uppermost will differ, and the speaker should take account of those differences. The beliefs that the communicator uses to elicit beliefs, as well as the beliefs that he might expect to change, will differ with the **sex** of the listener. And when audiences are composed of either men alone or women alone, these sex-related beliefs will be intensified.

3. That it is valid to suggest that different **ethnic and nationality** groups will hold different sets of beliefs has been demonstrated again and again. For example, an item in the paper recently indicated how different beliefs regarding the treatment of pregnancy are in Germany and in the United States. The article mentioned that German doctors do not urge the mother-to-be to drink milk but encourage her to drink light wines. Such differences could be repeated again and again in examples from all over the world. This variable may seem of little help to the speaker in the United States, however, where ethnic and nationality groups have all become mixed into a common culture. It is certainly true that we do have a common culture and that, on many issues, people in Seattle do not differ from those in Detroit or Miami. Nevertheless, almost all of us have a nationality identification of some type. We may have English, German, Japanese, Indian, or Italian grandparents or great-grandparents. Although we are all Americans, most families retain some practices and beliefs that tie us to the "old country." In many areas of the United States, these ties are strong, and the speaker who does not take them into account will not be successful. In Michigan, for example, there is a very strong Polish community living in Detroit. Former Governor G. Mennen Williams, a four-time winner of the gubernatorial chair, knew a great deal about the ideas and practices of these citizens, and much of his success can be traced to his ability to take account of their beliefs.

4. A few years ago, people could be separated very definitely on the basis of levels of **education** attained. Relatively few Americans had the opportunity to obtain more than a high-school education, and many millions could show only an eighth-grade diploma. The beliefs and disbeliefs of people with relatively little education seemed to differ greatly from those of college-educated individuals.

In particular, the central and intermediate beliefs of the college graduate were significantly different from those of the person with relatively little education.

Today, the picture has changed. More and more children go on to college, and almost all children obtain at least some high-school education. At all levels, children get a more uniform education. This means that differences in belief systems because of differences in education will be less dramatic. But there are still differences, and the communicator needs to take them into account when he can determine that a particular audience is composed entirely of college graduates or lacks college graduates altogether. The communicator may find that peripheral beliefs do not differ dramatically, but beliefs about authority and about the nature of the physical world might differ radically with the educational level of the audience.

5. An individual's **occupation** determines many of his beliefs. The social worker who works with juvenile delinquents, for example, is likely to have different beliefs about the treatment of teenagers than will the farmer who seldom sees a juvenile delinquent. The factory worker, operating a lathe in a machine shop, is likely to have a different set of beliefs about the treatment of the laborer than will the company's accountant, who never enters the plant.

In many respects, occupation is the best predictor of belief-disbelief systems that the communicator has. Unfortunately, except for the relatively rare situation in which the speaker knows that he is addressing a group from the same occupation, he is unable to make maximum use of this predictor of belief, because his audience will consist of people from many different occupations. When it is possible, however, a careful look at what an occupation entails about the possible belief systems of an individual holding that occupation will be extremely useful to the communicator.

6. Again, the **political-preference** variable is not useful in all situations. Furthermore, in the United States, the two major political parties do not differ so drastically that we can expect the central or perhaps even the intermediate belief systems to be very much different for a Republican than for a Democrat. However, there are specific peripheral beliefs on which the Republican party will differ from the Democratic party. If a communicator should be speaking to an audience with a majority of active members of a single party,

he should take this knowledge into account in predicting beliefs. For example, Democrats, in general, might be expected to be more in favor of federal aid to schools, or of federal assistance in social legislation, than would Republicans, in general.

7. **Religion** is much like political preference as a predictive variable. It certainly is a predictor of certain beliefs, but it is difficult to ascertain exactly what the religious composition of the audience might be. When the speaker knows that the audience is composed entirely of Lutherans, or Roman Catholics, or Methodists, he might look to the causes that these groups espouse, and the principles that they profess to believe in, as predictors for the probable beliefs of the audience. But when the audience is mixed, as it more frequently would be, the best he can do is to make an estimation of the general beliefs of Christians, compared with individuals of any other major sect, and attempt to ascertain whether it is likely that his audience is primarily composed of Christians, or of individuals from another major religious grouping. Even then, the religion of a listener is most likely to be reflected in the central way in which he views the physical world, or the way in which he views authority, than in the specific beliefs or disbeliefs he may hold about admitting communist China to the United Nations, or advocating federal aid to schools.

There are other variables that might help in predicting the belief structures of listeners, but the ones that have been discussed are certainly among the most helpful. One further point should be mentioned. The situation in which the listener is located probably has a great deal to do with his specific reaction to any speech. That is, when an individual is meeting with other members of his bowling club, the fact that he is also a Republican and a Methodist is probably less important in identifying parts of his belief structure than is his interest in bowling. The fact that the speaker is talking to a hospital auxiliary group, meeting at the hospital and calling for additional tax funds for hospital services, is probably more important in determining the beliefs of the audience members than the fact that some of the members are Roman Catholics or have a college education. In other words, peripheral beliefs in any specific situation may change somewhat depending on the other people present and the nature of the situation itself.

Summary

This chapter has suggested that beliefs are important to an understanding of the concept of proof, and of the role it plays in oral
communication. The speaker must know what his own beliefs are
and what beliefs he is interested in establishing or modifying in
his audience. The speaker must also be able to use the beliefs of
his audience to secure belief.

In describing beliefs, it was suggested that beliefs could be
looked at in terms of three levels of beliefs and disbeliefs, a central
level, an intermediate level, and a peripheral level. And it was
suggested that there were a number of variables that might help in
predicting what the beliefs of an audience might be, so that the
speaker can make use of an understanding of the concept of belief
in establishing the materials that will let him prove his case.

THREE

Proof and the speech situation

Analyzing beliefs, his own and those of his audience, helps the communicator in preparing his materials. It also points up the necessity for materials strong enough to establish his propositions to his auditors' satisfaction. A typical audience analysis will usually show a mixture of attitudes—some members will already be favorable toward the speaker's position, and others will be either neutral or negative. The communicator may find it strange that a large percentage of the individuals in any audience are not in agreement with him on any topic, even though they often seem to have access to the same information. He may ask: Why do different people develop different beliefs? How can the use of evidential materials change beliefs? What kind of belief changes can one expect from audiences? What role does the nature of our society play in determining the nature of communication? This chapter concentrates on these questions, in order to provide a basis for the emphasis on types and structures of evidence to be discussed in the second part of the book.

The speech communication process is usually taken for granted. We learn to speak at so early an age that we never ask what is involved in speech communication. Yet, the process can be described in many different ways. More than forty different descriptions of the communication process have appeared in print in various places, some of them more than two thousand years old. Writers have differed in their concentrations on the various levels of analysis of the communication process. One writer may confine himself to the social aspects of the communication process, another to the role of the mass media, and a third to the psychological principles involved in oral communication. In this volume, the interest is in proof and in building a model of the speech communication process. This model attempts to explain how individuals can be induced to change their beliefs and behaviors through the presentation of evidence in a communication situation. The analysis, however, must take place at several levels, because it is impossible to talk about the process as a whole. The rest of this chapter is concerned with the nature of the interaction between the speaker and his audience and the nature of responses in the speech communication situation, followed by an examination of the influence of society on speech communication.

Interaction: perception and production

An observer able to hide behind a one-way mirror and watch two people engaged in conversation might listen to that conversation and draw a picture of what is happening. He might include a speaker, a listener, and a set of MESSAGES that were being passed back and forth between the two. If he listened a bit longer, questions might occur to him. He might wonder where the speaker is getting the materials he is talking about or why the listener does not immediately agree with the speaker. He might even notice that the listener does not seem to be making any responses at all and infer that the speaker had been unsuccessful in his efforts.

A more relevant representation of the oral communication process in shown in Figure 1. It does not include all possible elements in that process, but it does detail some of the more important ingredients. The model shown in Figure 1 is an adaptation of some ideas about communication first advanced by Dean George Gerbner of the University of Pennsylvania.[1] It indicates that in any oral communication situation we have a SPEAKER, who PERCEIVES an event or series of events in the REAL WORLD, and arrives at a

[1]George Gerbner, "Toward a General Model of Communication," **Audio-Visual Communication Review,** IV (Summer 1956), 171–199.

Figure 1. Oral Communication

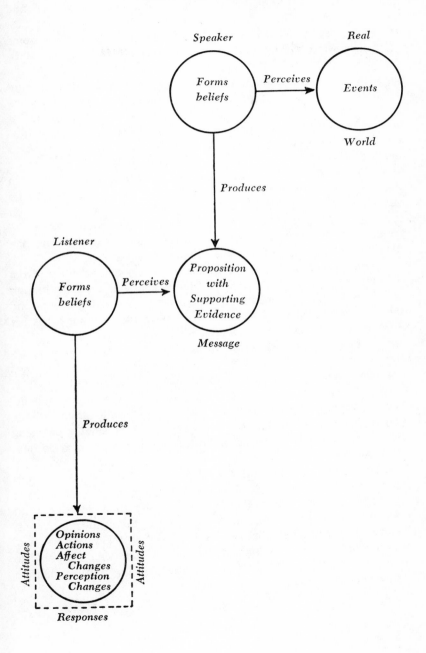

BELIEF about those events. He then PRODUCES a MESSAGE about his beliefs by organizing evidence around a proposition and then transmitting that message to a LISTENER or group of LISTENERS who again PERCEIVE the MESSAGE and take some position toward the message, a position indicated by the PRODUCTION of a RESPONSE to the message on the part of the listener. This basic process is found in all oral communication situations. Sometimes, the process will be complicated by the presence of more than one listener or more than one speaker. Sometimes, it will be complicated by having the message sent over radio or television, but the basic process of oral communication must occur much as diagramed.

The last half of this volume will be concerned specifically with the process of PRODUCTION, the ways in which evidence can be described and used in communication situations. The ways in which speakers and listeners tend to form beliefs have already been described. Now let us examine the process of perception and the nature of the responses that are available to the listener.

People are constantly made aware of events around them. From the time that, as new-born babies, they first notice a sound through all of their adult lives people are engaged in perceiving events and the stimuli coming from around them. One person cannot focus his attention on all possible stimulus objects. A writer sitting at his typewriter may be aware of only a few of the events that are occurring around him. He selects from those many events only the ones that seem important. Thus he does not notice the radio that is playing downstairs or the cars that travel in the street outside. People are not only capable of perceiving the world around them, and responding to it, but they possess a mechanism for choosing only those elements of the situation that are important at a particular time.

It is this selective process that makes individuals arrive at different conclusions, even after viewing the same scene. Thus if a group of people all view an attempted robbery, and then describe what happened, one person might have attended to the suspect's clothes, another to the weapon that he used, a third to the words he said, and a fourth to the condition of the victim. None would be able to report on the complete scene, even after looking at the situation several times.

In another situation, a group of people might observe several children coming home from school. One person concentrates on the child who runs across a lawn, and mutters something about hoodlums. Another perceives two boys scuffling and begins to talk about the school's failure to exercise control. A third looks at the dresses of the girls and comments on the probable income of parents who dress their children so expensively. Each person has observed essentially the same scene; but each person has selected from that scene what seems important to **him,** and his beliefs now reflect what he has perceived.

People have different beliefs, in part, because they have perceived different events. One cannot experience the daily events of an individual living in another city or another country. He cannot have the same beliefs as someone from another country or another city, or even from the same city. Actually, even when we are all looking at the same event, different beliefs may result from our perception, because we are all motivated differently. What gets **in,** via the perceptual process, is in part determined by personal internal states. There are many such internal states, and only a few are listed below, but they are enough to indicate how widely differing beliefs can be developed.

If I am hungry, I am likely to select and concentrate on events in the perceptual world that might lead to food. I will be more attracted to pictures of food, the smells of cooking, or the sound of the dinner bell. After eating, I may pass completely over a picture of a juicy steak in a magazine, and if asked whether I saw the picture, I might say no. Hunger is only one **biological motive, or drive.** Others include thirst, pain avoidance, and sex. These drives may not be so important in determining beliefs as some that we learn, but they still remain as powerful indicators of behavior. They can be the determining factor in what is perceived, and thus in what is believed, by an individual.

Every child, regardless of his nationality, spends a lot of his time in learning to value certain behaviors. For example, the child may be taught that he has a duty to be loyal to his country. When he grows up, this may lead to his volunteering for military service as the result of hearing a speech in which the speaker appealed to a motive of loyalty. Or the child may hear certain comments about the traditional customs of his family. He may grow up to place high value on conformity and would respond to speech materials attempting to support a proposition by referring to what people did in the past, or to what the majority of people think about the problem.

There are many **learned motives,** and from them one learns the culture from which an individual comes, as well as what his family life is like, and the stimuli to which he will respond. Common learned motives in the United States include desires for social participation, honor, loyalty, competition, and conformity. In other countries, the strength of the competition motive, for example, may not be as strong as it is in the United States, and a speaker might have to emphasize different motives in order to be a successful communicator.

Motives work in two directions. Not only are they important in determining what message an individual will attend to in the first place, but they further help to determine how the individual will respond after he makes the decision to attend to the message. Thus perception depends not only on the physical equipment which the individual possesses—the eyes, ears, sense of touch, and so forth—but also on the state of the individual's biological drives and his learned motives.

The psychologist is fond of saying that when a stimulus has been perceived by an individual, a response will follow. The speaker, however, is frequently faced with the situation in which a speech has been made without a discernible reaction from the audience. Has he failed in his purpose? Not necessarily. Figure 1 suggests that there are at least four types of responses that the listener might make to any message. One might expect **opinion** changes, **perception** changes, **affect** changes, or **action** changes. Opinion changes can be defined as changes in what the individual says after the speech. An individual might say, "I think that the speaker has a real point to make." This would be a change in opinion that could be attributed to the results of the listener's hearing the message.

A perception change occurs when the listener changes the way in which he tends to view the problem. For example, a listener might be exposed to a speech on the population explosion. He listens, and, as a result of the speech, he now begins reading every article he can find on the subject. He may say nothing about the speech, nor does he seem to do anything. But there has been some effect of the speech, because the individual has changed the way in which he views the world. There has been a perception change.

Affect changes are changes in the emotional state of the listener. Probably there is nothing more difficult to define or detect than a change in an individual's emotional state. Nevertheless, many listeners have experienced a change in feeling toward a speaker—to a feeling of sympathy for him or to a dislike for him and what he seems to represent. These are affect changes, changes in the emotional condition of the listener.

Finally, the last observable change in the audience is an actual change in overt behavior. The listener reaches into his pocket to donate money to the speaker's cause. Or he goes into the voting booth to vote for the candidate favored by the communicator. Action changes are the results most desired by speakers, and the hardest to obtain. It is frequently easy to induce some emotional response in an individual, or even to get him to say that he is in favor of the position advocated by the communicator. But to get the individual to do what is being recommended to him is difficult.

All observable communication effects take place against a pattern of attitude change on the part of the listener. We cannot see when an individual has changed an attitude, because attitudes are nonobservable. But when an observable change of any kind takes place, this **means** that an attitude change has occurred. It is possible, however, to have attitude changes without their being followed by observable changes in opinions, emotions, perceptions, or actions. From a consideration of attitude changes of varying degrees, the process can be traced by which an individual decides to adopt a new idea that has been presented to him. The process entails five steps: **attention, interest, trial, evaluation,** and **adoption.**

For any communicator to be successful, he must first have the attention of the people to whom he is talking. To achieve this, he will have to present materials that can give the listener a reason for listening. He may not need complete proof at this stage, but he will need materials to make the listener select the message he is producing as one worthy of attention. The second step, more difficult than getting the attention of the audience, is arousing their interest in the problem. Most of us have spent time listening to a speech, and attended to it, but have left the situation with little real interest in what the speaker is saying. Again, the speaker will need to provide enough evidence to let the listener feel that he **should** be concerned about the problem, that it affects him or the things that concern him. Attention and interest go hand in hand, and they are generally the easiest reactions to secure from the audience in a communication situation. However, many communicators may decide that they have been successful in accomplishing specific changes in behavior when they have only succeeded in getting auditors to show that they are interested in the topic. Attention and interest are prerequisites to success, but they are not the entire story.

The last three steps, trial, evaluation and adoption, are more difficult to accomplish. After the speaker has people interested in the new topic or the new idea, he will require more communication, using more materials, to get an auditor to try the new idea. The listener may be interested in something new, but if a trial will require particular efforts or monetary expenditures, the level of proof obtained by the communicator must be higher than that required to get the listener's attention or interest. Assuming that the speaker has been successful in getting a listener to try the new idea once—"try it on for size"—he must communicate the necessity of making some evaluation of the trial. Again, the communication may have to include possible criteria for evaluation, standards for evaluation, and methods of evaluation. To use a homely example, if one gets a farmer to plant some new bean variety, he must then show the farmer how to compare the old variety with the new variety. Finally, assuming that the individual has made an evaluation favoring the new idea, further communication may still be needed in order to convince him that adoption of the new idea on a permanent basis will be helpful. Many people "know what is good for them" but may cling to old habits and ideas out of simple unwillingness to abandon them. Additional proof may need to be supplied even at this stage in the process.

The influence of society on speech communication

The model of the communication process diagramed in Figure 1 could easily suggest that communication occurs in a vacuum. The diagram suggests that speakers produce messages, which are transmitted to listeners, who then respond. The diagram does not indicate the many other factors that tend to help determine the nature of the communication that takes place, the constraints placed on the communication situation itself, or the role that other sources of communication play in determining the effects of communication.

Speech communication can take place under many circumstances: a chat across the back fence with a neighbor, a few comments over a cup of coffee with a friend in a restaurant, casual remarks at a meeting of a Girl Scout committee, a formal speech at a national convention, a nationwide address of the President over all possible types of mass media. Most people do not engage in nationwide addresses, nor even in speeches to national conventions. They do speak to their neighbors, and they will probably make some remarks to the social and civic groups to which they belong. Perhaps more important than the speaking they might do, however, is the listening they do. Because, in a very real sense, it is that listening that determines what they will say in future situations. It is the information taken in through reception of messages produced by others that determines what one will believe in and thus what he will offer as evidence when he wishes to secure responses from other people.

To suggest that communication can take place in many different types of situations, is to suggest that the social situation in which communication occurs is a variable important to the speaker's success. What an individual might be willing to do or believe in one situation, is not what he would be willing to do or believe in another. When one is alone with a speaker, it is sometimes easier to respond to his statements than when one is seated in the middle of a large auditorium surrounded by many other people. A very good example of the constraints that a social situation can place on a listener is the typical response to the speaker's request "Does anyone have any questions?" Many of us have sat in an auditorium and watched a group of people respond to that question by saying nothing. The speaker might well feel that his message was completely understood. However, it is more likely that the presence of many people in the group has prevented anyone from asking what he thinks may be a "stupid question." Watch what happens after the speech. Frequently, individuals will come up and **then** begin asking questions. The presence of other people in the oral communication situation does place some social constraints on the types of responses that are likely to be made.

Constraints work in more than one way, however. It is easier to say no when the speaker and auditor are alone, than when they are joined by other people and the listener feels social pressure to take the activity recommended by the speaker. Many of us have had the experience of being asked to help with some civic project. If we were asked during a meeting at which other members of the association were present, it was difficult to say no. Even though we would experience no punishments, nor be ostracized from the group, we felt pressure to do what had been asked. On the other hand, if the same request was made of us, phrased in exactly the same words, in a telephoned message, the social pressure was largely gone. We could say no to requests like these with little of the feelings of social pressure encountered in the group situation.

The speaker must analyze the nature of the social situation in which he will be talking just as well as he analyzes the nature of the individuals who will be in the situation. A failure to realize that people will not take certain kinds of suggestions because of the presence or absence of other individuals, can mean a failure of the communicator to accomplish his intent. It is always difficult to generalize about what responses can be expected in what kinds of situations, but a few suggestions can be made:

1. When social pressure exists that would tend to operate contrary to a speaker's intent, the presence of a group is likely to be inhibiting to the speaker.

2. When the speaker is advocating a position that is in line with the majority of the audience, the presence of the audience will tend to facilitate the speaker's purpose and bring dissident members of the audience into line.

3. When the intent of the speaker is to produce action on the part of individual audience members, the presence of the audience may help to reduce the pressures that would normally lead one to refuse to take such action.

4. When the speaker's intent is to change attitudes in a direction away from the commonly accepted norms for a proposition, the presence of an audience that **shows agreement** with the speaker will facilitate audience acceptance of such change. On the other hand, if the audience does not show agreement, response is inhibited for audience members who might tend to agree with the speaker. (This is why "ringers" or "shills" are sometimes placed in an audience.)

5. A speaker who intends to obtain a response that merely indi-cates agreement with his position is perhaps more likely to secure it when only one listener is present. But a positive response to a request for specific action may be easier to secure when other audi-ence members are also agreeing to take similar actions.

These five suggestions describe only a few of those situations that the speaker might encounter. But they should indicate that commu-nication will take place within some particular social environment, and either in the presence or the absence of other people. A speak-er's attempt to provide proof for his proposition may depend for its success on the nature of the social situation. One can secure responses in a church that he cannot secure at a Kiwanis luncheon. He can secure responses when he has the listener alone that would be difficult to obtain when he is facing the same listener and 499 other listeners. A speaker must make as careful an analysis of the social situation in which communication is taking place as he does of the other elements of the situation.

Summary

This chapter has suggested that the concept of proof must be re-lated to the entire communication process. It suggested a model of that process based on the major concepts of perception of an event and production of messages and responses concerning that event. It suggested that perception is selective and dependent on the needs, desires, memories, and past experiences of the communicator and listener. It suggested that responses are all based on maintenance of or change in attitudes, which underlie any changes in opinion, per-ception, emotions, or actions. A hierarchy of responses in terms of difficulty of achievement by the speaker was suggested, indicating that that hierarchy ranged from awareness and interest to trial, evaluation, and adoption. Finally, it suggested that communication does not take place within a vacuum, but rather occurs within a particular social environment, with varying numbers of people present. The nature of the evidence needed by the speaker to prove his case, and the amount of that evidence, are determined in large part by the kind of response desired, and the situation in which it is desired.

FOUR

Substantive proof: evidence

One of the most interesting characteristics of people is their eagerness to transmit their ideas to other people. Think over the last two- or three-day period and ask yourself how many times you talked to someone else about some idea you had. How many times did someone talk to you about an idea he had? Whether you are talking or listening to someone else, the chances are that ideas will form the basis for the messages you send or receive. The problem is that ideas may be either good or bad.

Some time ago, the author's young son appeared before his desk and announced that "I have an idea." Asked what his idea was, he said that he wanted to use his water-color paints to "paint pretty pictures on my bedroom walls." Most parents would classify this idea, coming from a five-year-old, as a bad idea. My son's support for his idea was that it would save money on pictures, and he knows that saving money ranks high with most adults. He had tested the adequacy of the idea before he attempted to communicate to an auditor. My answer that we did not need to save money "that much," probably puzzled the young communicator, but it represented the other side of the proof situation. I, too, had evaluated the idea, and found it inadequate.

The first chapter of this book, in defining proof as the process of using evidence to test ideas, did not stress that ideas are tested in at least two places in a typical communication situation. The communicator who gets an idea must test the adequacy of that idea before he transmits it. The auditors must test the idea again through their evaluation of the evidence presented by the communicator. The following discussion of various modes of proof—substantive, logical, and emotional—thus has two values. It is concerned with the ways in which the communicator arrives at a position on matters of public policy. And it is concerned with the ways in which a communicator might present his position to an audience so that they, too, will arrive at the same position.

A concept of evidence

It might seem relatively easy to discuss the concept of evidence, and discuss it from the standpoints of both the communicator and the audience. An example points out some of the problems. In the United States today, a number of people claim to have seen "spaceships" land, and to have seen "small, green men" emerge from the spaceships. Some have even claimed to have talked to the "small, green men." These people have told others about their experiences and have been disbelieved. Why have they been disbelieved? After all, they are presenting evidence for their views, purportedly the evidence of their own eyes. Many of these people seem quite sincere in their statements that they have seen the objects and the people they describe. But when they report their experiences to others, they are not believed. What was "proof" for the communicator was not "proof" for the auditor.

Spaceships and little green men comprise an extreme example of the problem that plagues every court of law and every policy maker in any legislature. What does constitute adequate evidence for the support of any proposition? What kind of evidence is necessary to satisfy every member of an audience that the ideas presented are adequate? In one sense, these questions can never be answered. It is probably impossible to set up proof for any proposition in such a way that every possible auditor will accept the proposition. Even in a case as well documented as the assassination of President Kennedy, there remains a small group of people who vehemently maintain that Lee Harvey Oswald was not the individual firing the murder weapon. They are not satisfied with the evidence that was offered to support the main proposition. One can, however, work to identify clearly the types of evidence available for use, and the ways in which these types of evidence can be used to support any proposition.

Although the term evidence is, in general, used to refer to any attempt to support a proposition, its use in this volume is limited to **statements of fact.** The discussion will be concerned with categorizing statements about the real world in terms of their applicability to general propositions. The description of evidence states the relation that a statement of fact bears to a general proposition.

For the legal profession, evidence has been used to refer to **any** means by which an alleged matter of fact is established or disproved. This might include inferences drawn from statements of fact, the testimony of expert witnesses, confessions, and the like. The rules developed by the lawyer to determine whether a particular piece of evidence should be admitted for consideration are complicated. They have been refined over a period of centuries and are concerned only with the establishment of the truth of a statement of fact.

The typical speech communicator, however, usually is more interested in deciding what stand he will take on a question of public policy than he does on a question of fact. He may be interested in deciding whether his community should build a swimming pool, or whether a particular political candidate is the better man, or whether the United States should support the government of Viet Nam. These are statements that express an idea about future activities and are clearly different from statements about the guilt of an individual being tried for robbery. But the same kinds of evidence are used to support questions of policy as are used to support the questions of fact with which a court is concerned. And a consideration of the ways in which the lawyer classifies evidence will further an understanding of the use of evidence in the consideration of policy questions.

Types of evidence

It is impossible to categorize evidence in such a way that the categories do not overlap to some extent. The classification chosen here is one that is relatively simple, but more helpful to the average communicator than a more complicated system.

Direct evidence is a statement that is immediately and directly related to the question under consideration. Thus, in a trial in an accident case, a witness may state, "I saw the car hit the little girl." This is direct evidence, a statement that represents knowledge gained from use of the senses, and that is immediately related to the issue in question.

In considering a policy question, direct evidence might consist of some event that is personally witnessed. For example, a driver, proceeding over a well-traveled bridge, might see the car ahead, swerving to miss a hole in the roadbed, hit the retaining wall. His observation might well serve as sufficient evidence to argue that the county commissioner ought to get the roadbed repaired. Another example of the use of direct evidence might come from the man who was robbed while walking home from the bus through a dark area, and who subsequently argues for the installation of street lights. Similarly, a speaker may be convinced that better fire protection is necessary when it takes the fire department twenty-five minutes to get to his burning home. Each of these situations is concerned with materials arrived at through the senses—seeing, hearing, touching, tasting, and smelling—representing evidence that the communicator believes is directly related to the policy question under consideration.

It should be noted, however, that the situations mentioned above are concerned with evidence that has been obtained by the communicator. It is quite likely that an auditor may not see the importance or relevancy of the evidence, nor will an auditor be as concerned with something that happens to the speaker as is the speaker. If I am listening to you argue for street lights, and have not been robbed, I may be inclined to depreciate your evidence and say that what happened was "an isolated case." Or an auditor might argue that the evidence is certainly true, but that it does not support the proposition that the speaker says it does. Thus, a listener might argue that the fire department is not at fault because it took twenty-five minutes to get to the scene of the action; the fault lies with the poor access roads leading to the burning house. He might argue that what is needed is not better fire protection, but better roads. Again, no one has disputed the truth of the statements of fact that make up the evidence, but they believe that it is not adequate support for the question of policy the speaker is interested in. The fact that auditors can and do question the applicability of evidence to questions of .fact, means that the communicator will have to be sure that his evidence is as complete as he can make it.

In many cases, there are no eye-witness accounts of an event. Yet people may be convinced that the event occurred. They become so because of the presence of **indirect,** or **circumstantial, evidence.** In a legal situation, one might have the following report:

> I saw John Smith knocking at Jerry Green's door. When the door opened, Smith rushed into the house and slammed the door after him. About ten minutes later, I heard a rather loud noise, and then Smith came running out of the house. He ran to his car and drove away. It looked to me as if he had a gun in his hand, so I called the police.

If the police find that Jerry Green has indeed been shot, observers would probably be inclined to agree that there is a strong suspicion that Smith fired the fatal shot. They cannot be positive, because no one saw the shot fired, but the evidence might well tend to convince them that Smith is guilty. This kind of evidence is indirect or circumstantial evidence.

Several years ago, a group of teen-agers was killed in the early hours of the morning after a graduation party. The incident shocked the entire city. Parents began making speeches at various civic functions, advocating that more direct control be taken at graduation parties by school officials and by the parents themselves. The parents argued that the victims had obtained liquor and that this was the reason for the fatal accident. No one had seen the accident, and there was no one who could testify directly to the fact that the teen-agers had been drinking. The evidence linking the accident to the drinking was strictly circumstantial. But the evidence, though indirect, was strong enough to convince the school system and parents that better control must be exerted over graduation activities. Here is an example of the use of circumstantial evidence to support a statement of public policy.

Direct evidence can sometimes be attributed to more than one proposition, and indirect evidence is even more likely to be so attributed. In the example just cited, it is certainly possible to argue that the teen-agers' deaths could be related to the sale of liquor in the city, or to the inspection of automobiles for safety, or to the necessity for an increased police force. In some circumstances, indirect evidence is all that is available in attempting to make an assessment of a question of policy, but, if this is so, it should be remembered that the case must be made much stronger. This is particularly true when a number of alternative courses of action are available to an auditor. If a speaker decides that a particular course of action is the best available, then he must be sure that the weight of the evidence he is using points to the course of action he has selected, and not to some other course of action that might be advocated by another communicator.

Direct evidence is linked in a positive manner to the question under consideration. But sometimes it is impossible to find evidence that is linked directly to a proposition. In such a situation, it may be necessary to support the proposition by showing that it is impossible to support its opposite. For example, Negro leaders argue that there is discrimination in housing in the North, because there are no Negroes living in white neighborhoods. This is **negative evidence.** Negroes might not be living in certain places for many reasons, but discrimination is frequently difficult to prove with direct, positive evidence. Thus, it is necessary to turn to negative evidence.

Negative evidence is not always admissible in U. S. courts. Yet we all use negative evidence to conduct much of our daily life, and our business institutions depend highly on negative evidence. When the government wants to make a security check on an individual who is applying for a position in a sensitive agency, one piece of evidence that is always checked for is a police record. If no police record exists, the assumption is made that the individual is honest. When a company wants to hire a new employee, they might go through the same check with school officials and the police. Failure to have a police record is almost always equated with being an acceptable candidate.

Clearly, any of the decisions made as a result of considering negative evidence are open to serious question. Just because a man does not have a police record is no guarantee that he is honest. The speech communicator ought to be extremely careful of negative evidence. He ought to be careful both in his dependence on such evidence in making his own decisions, and in using such evidence in communicating ideas to an audience.

Much of the evidence used in public speaking must come from

materials gathered by others. Usually, the speaker who is trying to decide which side to support on a policy question is not able to view all of the evidence for himself. He must turn to the reported experiences of others in order to obtain enough evidence. Some of that evidence will be given by individuals whose best interest will be served if the policy question is decided in a particular way. The evidence, then, works to their best advantage. But in other cases, the evidence will come from someone whose interests will be served only if the question is decided in a way opposite to that in which the evidence seems to point. These individuals are said to be giving **reluctant evidence**.

In a criminal case, the defendant might take the stand and admit that he was near the scene of the crime at the time when the crime was supposed to have taken place. This would be reluctant evidence, because it clearly would be to the interest of the defendant to have been able to show that he was far away from the scene of the crime. In matters of public policy, a public official might testify that his department is not run as efficiently as he would hope. Several years ago, a newspaper in a Midwestern city reported that certain food stores were adulterating their hamburger with horse meat and making much larger profits. In the ensuing discussion, the head of the city health department admitted that stores were not inspected very often and that when they were, only a cursory glance was given to the products in them. This testimony resulted in stronger laws against adulteration and a complete revamping of the inspection system, including the dismissal of the head of the health department. Here, reluctant evidence resulted in drastic changes.

Most people are inclined to place considerable weight on evidence coming from a reluctant witness, although it may be no more true than evidence that is not reluctant. But the credibility of the witness seems to most of us to be better established when he is testifying against what seem to be his best interests.

Evidence that consists of things is called **real evidence**. Real evidence includes photographs, movies, X rays, maps, diagrams, experiments, or physical objects. In deciding a question of fact, a jury may be shown a gun that convinces them that a particular individual was guilty of a crime. Or a picture may be shown that convinces an observer that a building was in very poor condition. In law, particularly in jury trials, the introduction of real evidence is extremely important. Its importance lies in the ability of a judge or a jury to "see for themselves."

It is a little more difficult for the communicator interested in a policy question to make use of real evidence. But in some situations real, physical evidence can be brought to bear in support of a particular policy question. For example, imagine that the quality of construction of a particular sidewalk by a city crew responsible for laying new sidewalks and curbs has been questioned. The speech communicator might decide for himself whether the sidewalks are in good shape by making a direct inspection of a number of places on the questioned sidewalk. If he does find it to be in poor condition, that will tend to fix his own decision. He must now communicate his decision to an auditor or series of auditors. He might do so with a picture of the sidewalks or of a diagram of the cracks that extended throughout the concrete, or he might bring in a piece of the crumbling concrete and pass it around among his auditors. In each case, the communicator would be using real evidence and making the point in a way that is difficult to make as effectively in any other way.

In 1962 refugees escaping from Cuba offered evidence that the Russians had begun building missile sites on Cuba. The evidence consisted of eyewitness statements about such construction. This evidence was apparently gathered and evaluated. But it was not until photo-reconnaissance planes brought back pictures of the missile sites under construction that the government took direct action. Eyewitness accounts were important, but the availability of real evidence was decisive.

When man first created written languages, he made it possible to create evidence that could be used later to support propositions that might arise. Evidence can be created for the specific purpose of being used as evidence. **Created evidence** may be contrasted with accidental evidence, materials that were not prepared to be used as evidence, but that have been discovered.

The lawyer has used created evidence for centuries. Documents such as wills, notes, mortgages, and contracts are prepared so that evidence will be available if a question ever arises about the problem under consideration. Such created evidence has an advantage in that it can be placed in written form and checked for accuracy even after the passage of many years. A second advantage is that such evidence can be made specific to a particular question and is thus not so likely to be attributed to some other proposition.

In policy questions, created evidence is frequently used. Indeed, many newsmen have commented on the frequency with which public officials create evidence for later use. A question of public policy is likely to arise, and a proponent asks an official to make a statement that he can use in the discussion over the policy. For example, anticipating a legislative discussion over school aid, the superintendent of public instruction for the state may release information on the state of school-district finances. This material will then be used in the legislative discussion as evidence. The superintendent, knowing that the question will arise in the legislature, has created appropriate evidence ahead of time.

It might seem that more reliance should be placed in accidental evidence than in evidence that is created for a specific purpose. And it is certainly true that evidence might have been created in such a way that only one side of the situation has been presented. On the other hand, created evidence may tell a more precise story because it was created with the particular question in mind. Accidental evidence, while seeming to bear more weight with the typical auditor, may have been gathered or stated in such a fashion that it can be applied to several questions, not only to the one under consideration.

Each of the types of evidence just discussed could be applied to many different kinds of questions. Strictly speaking, it would be most desirable for us to have direct, firsthand knowledge of all the events pertaining to any given question of public policy and to be able to show real evidence to any audience about our decision. In practice, of course, the average citizen does not have the time or the means to absorb first-hand all the information available on even a minor matter of public policy. For example, suppose that the proposition is made to increase school taxes to pay for more teachers and thus relieve crowded conditions. The average citizen might go to one school in the city and look in a classroom window to see whether it is crowded. If he is really concerned, he might go to several schools and repeat the experiment. But to do so he must be able to leave his own job during the middle of the day, to observe every classroom, and to assimilate all the evidence he receives. For most people, such a program is impossible.

If it is impossible to observe personally all aspects of a situation or of a question, the average person must take the next best course. He must depend on evidence that has been collected and arranged by others. For most questions of public policy, the communicator must evaluate evidence much as the people he will later speak to will evaluate it. He will be dependent for information on hearsay materials, on evidence that he has not been able to verify personally. This means that any tests for the adequacy of evidence must also include tests for determining the adequacy of the reporter of the evidence.

Tests of evidence

Any time a piece of evidence is used to support a proposition, the evidence should be tested. It should fit the proposition under consideration. It should be complete, its originator should be competent to report evidence, and all conflicting evidence available should be accounted for. Some of the tests for determining whether a proposition has or has not been supported will be discussed in Chapter 5. But three kinds of tests can be applied to any statement of fact in order to determine its adequacy as evidence. These are the tests of relevancy, materiality, and competence.

Many of us, in listening to a speaker, have discovered that he seems to be giving us information that has little or no relationship to the problem under discussion. The author once listened to a speaker in a public meeting who was speaking in favor of a tight curfew on teen-agers. His evidence for such a curfew was that every afternoon, after the local high school closed its doors, a "mob of kids" rode past his house in their "hotrods" and made an excessive amount of noise. His evidence was impressive. He was an actual eyewitness to the scenes he had described. Unfortunately, the evidence he was presenting had absolutely nothing to do with the question of whether teen-agers should be allowed out after 10 p.m. The presence of teen-agers in an automobile at three o'clock in the afternoon is not relevant to the question of a ten o'clock curfew.

The question of a curfew is a policy matter, but **relevancy** is just as important when one is considering complicated questions of fact. For example, suppose that one wished to establish that the price of automobiles has increased over the past twenty years. In order to establish it fully, he might wish to show that the price of an automobile has increased faster than the cost of living has increased. This would give a much better case than mere evidence that a Ford costs $125 more than it did twenty years ago. In such a case, it would be perfectly appropriate to introduce evidence comparing the current price of a pound of steak, butter, or chicken with that of the earlier period. These items of evidence become relevant with the introduction of the relationship between automobile price and the cost of living, currently and twenty years ago.

Relevancy may well seem like a simple matter. Any given piece of evidence either is or is not relevant to the question under discussion. Making a decision about relevancy, however, may be extremely difficult. In the case of the teen-age curfew already cited, a number of people obviously believed that the statements about teen-age behavior in the afternoon **were** relevant to teen-age behavior at night. Several auditors seemed to have made their decision to support the curfew proposal on the basis of the speech described.

It is easy to take an experience one has had and apply it as evidence to a problem. For many policy questions, direct, relevant evidence may be difficult to obtain, and the temptation is great to apply irrelevant evidence in an attempt to arrive at a decision about the problem. The speaker must exercise great care to avoid the application of irrelevant materials to the problems he is considering.

On many questions, literally hundreds of small bits of evidence will be available. Some of the evidence may seem significant to the question, and some may seem related, if only remotely so. We say that evidence is **material** to a question when it is significantly related to the question; as the degree of relationship becomes more and more tenuous, we say that the evidence becomes more and more **immaterial.**

The example cited before of U. S. behavior during the Cuban crisis of 1962 illustrates the importance of the question of materiality to decision-making and subsequent speech communication. For many months, Cuban refugees had issued a steady stream of reports that the Russians were helping the Castro regime build a series of missile sites. These reports were clearly relevant to any possible U. S. decision. But it was not until he had clear photographic evidence that President John F. Kennedy made a final decision to force removal of any missiles in Cuba and communicated his decision to the world. The photographic evidence was considered to be both relevant and material. The reports were certainly relevant, but, for the President, they did not form a sufficiently clear picture to be considered material.

In legal situations, materiality may be determined in order to avoid the introduction of evidence that might only cloud the main issues in the case. Suppose a man is accused of stealing a crate of oranges. When the case comes to trial, the defendant's attorney might try asking a witness whether he knows what color an orange is. The chances are that this evidence would be considered immaterial. Whether the witness knows the color of an orange could be relevant to the case, but the court might decide that it is not material to the main trial issue. In essence, the court would be saying that there might be a relationship between the evidence presented and the trial issue, but that any relationship is tenuous at best and should not be allowed to cloud the main issue.

In an area of concern to the average speaker, much of the same type of reasoning might be applied to considerations of evidence. Many small bits of data could well apply to the issue under consideration, but it is frequently better to pass over these minor pieces of evidence to concentrate on the major items of evidence related to the topic.

In the legal situation, evidence is not considered admissible unless it is declared to be **competent.** To be considered competent, the evidence must be both adequate and sufficient to establish the point under consideration. For example, a layman would not be allowed to testify concerning the medical cause of death. A witness might testify that he saw Sam shoot Jim, but it would take a physician's testimony to establish that Jim died from gunshot wounds in the chest. A photograph that is blurred, or that gives evidence of having been tampered with, would not be admitted as evidence. If it could be shown that a prospective witness was under the influence of alcohol at the time his observations took place, his testimony would probably not be taken seriously. In each of these situations, the evidence is not competent.

When moving from questions of fact in the legal situation to a consideration of policy questions, competency is still important. But some of the grounds on which competency is determined must change. When one concerns himself with policy questions, he is usually concerned with the competency of the **individuals** providing information. Not the evidence alone, but the competency of the individual providing the evidence, concerns him. In other words, he must consider the **credibility** of the witness.

The concern with credibility takes two forms. The people who supply the evidence used to make decisions are important. So is the way in which the speaker appears to his listeners. A number of questions can be asked to help determine whether an individual is competent—remember that auditors ask themselves the same questions about a speaker that the speaker asks about his informants.

1. Is the individual in a position to have access to the information? When a speaker declares that a traffic light is needed at a particular corner because small children have been hit at the corner, his listeners are more likely to place faith in the testimony of an individual living close to the corner than in one who has never been near the corner. When the issue is foreign policy toward a particular country, the listener is more inclined to place confidence in someone who has been in the country than in someone who has not. Regarding access to information, however, remember that just being present does not guarantee accurate information. An old experiment that is still run in many college classrooms indicates this. The class will be sitting and listening to a lecture, when the door opens, and a person runs down in front of the stage and fires a gun at the professor. Then he runs out of the room. The professor falls down, then gets up, explains that it was all a joke, and asks the class to write an account of the incident. Even though all the people in the class were watching and saw the incident, each person will report something different. We all tend to see what we expect to see, and this selective perception means that we cannot always depend on being able to accept evidence merely because an individual was apparently in a position to observe an incident.

2. Is the individual knowledgeable in the area under consideration? If a community is considering the building of a new sewage plant, opposition testimony might be presented on the grounds that "The water tastes all right, so why are we worried about a new sewage system?" If this testimony is opposed by that of the city health director, who testifies that "The new sewage system is needed because our tests show that dangerous bacteria are showing up in the drinking water supplied from the city wells," the residents

would probably be inclined to trust the health director's testimony. He would be considered more competent than a layman on the particular question. An "expert" is particularly important when the acquisition of evidence requires some interpretation. When concerned with public health, one consults officials in that area. Education issues call for expert consultants in education. Even with the best of intentions, an individual who is completely untrained in an area might have difficulty interpreting what he is observing.

3. Is the individual reporting all the available evidence? It is extremely easy to select only the evidence that seems to support a particular side. Even when the individual is not being "fooled" into selective perception, he finds it difficult to remember everything that occurred. Eye-witnesses tend to remember those portions of an event that seem to fulfill their own expectations; they may not report all the details necessary for a communicator to make up his own mind about some question.

In judging the competency of an individual, one must be able to estimate whether or not he is reporting all of the available evidence. If one makes an estimate and is wrong, it could well mean that he will find himself deciding to support one side of a question, when he should have supported the other side. In communicating a decision to others, a speaker may find himself communicating an incomplete set of evidence, which may have the effect of his being judged as incompetent.

Each of the questions mentioned is designed to help the communicator establish the competency of the evidence he is evaluating. If the communicator is not able to "see for himself," then he must establish the competency of the sources on which he is relying. And after he does make a determination regarding the competency of his sources, and makes a policy decision regarding some question, he must realize that he, too, will be judged by his auditors in the same manner as that in which he judges his original informants.

Summary

This chapter has suggested that evidence is all around us. No matter what the question might be, a matter of fact, or a question of policy, the speaker must depend on evidence in order to make up his own mind and in order to be successful in communicating ideas to a set of auditors. The communicator may choose from several different types of evidence: direct, indirect, negative, reluctant, real, or created. The type of evidence available depends on the nature of the question to be asked and the relation of the communicator to the necessary evidence. The communicator may have to depend entirely on others if the topic concerns foreign policy, whereas he himself may have direct knowledge about his community's needs.

Once a source of evidence is found, it must be judged for the adequacy and completeness of the evidence it makes available. The criteria suggested for this evaluation are the three grounds of relevancy, materiality, and competency. When judging evidence, the communicator should keep in mind that there are two aspects of evidence. He must judge the adequacy of the available evidence in order to make accurate decisions on his own, and he must also be concerned with the way in which any available evidence is likely to appear to an audience.

FIVE

Logical proof: inference

Definitions

A single piece of evidence may establish the truth or falsity of a proposition. An eyewitness account of a shooting may be the only evidence needed to convict the shooter. A single accident at a dangerous corner may be sufficient to mobilize community action. A school fire may lead to changes in the fire regulations for an entire state. Each of these is an example of situations in which a single piece of evidence is used to support another proposition. A more usual situation, however, is that in which the communicator is faced by many pieces of data and has to arrive at a conclusion that will be consistent with all of them.

In order to draw conclusions successfully, to explain, or to predict, the communicator must make use of the **inferential process.** He must take the evidence that he has accumulated, place it into some structural arrangement, and determine exactly what proposition can be inferred as a result of examination of the structural arrangement. Before examining some of the structural arrangements that philosophers and scientists have developed, it is interesting to note just how important inferences are to speech communication. Any time a statement is made about the unknown, it must be an inference. Each of the following statements is an inference, a **statement made about what will occur or should occur in the future:**

1. It will rain in Michigan tomorrow.
2. The President will be re-elected for a second full term.
3. The United Nations will live to celebrate its fortieth anniversary.
4. There will be another World War within the next five years.
5. Man will land on the moon before 1970.

Each of these statements is an inference. None of them is capable of immediate verification, although eventually all of them can be verified. None of the statements was made "off the top of the head"; there is solid data that can be used to make each of the inferences cited. Spend a few minutes thinking back over the last week and try to remember the number of times you used an inference in speaking to someone else. You probably made at least one statement asserting something about the future in almost every extended conversation.

Statements about the future are only one kind of inference. Another important kind of inference is the **generalization,** a statement that draws together a number of observations. The following are examples of inferences that generalize:

1. College students at Michigan State University come from the top quarter of their high-school graduating class.
2. The United States always wins the wars it enters.
3. Women have a longer life span than men.
4. Most Americans do not attend church regularly.
5. Children who are good readers have more access to books than do poor readers.

Generalizations take individual pieces of evidence and attempt to draw a conclusion that is representative of the entire set of statements. One would decide that the inference about winning wars is correct if he looked into history, determined the number of times the United States engaged in war, and determined the number of times the United States won the war. If he finds that every war that the United States entered, it won, then he would be entitled to make the generalization that "The United States always wins the wars it enters."

A third type of inference is the statement that requires an **explanation.** Frequently, such inferences are phrased as a question, but the intention is clearly inferential, because the author is usually interested in the "why" or the "because" of a statement. Such questions include:

1. Why did North Korea attack South Korea?
2. What causes icebergs?
3. What is the relationship between gun ownership and suicide?
4. What causes cancer?
5. Why does the United States have such a high unemployment rate?

As they are phrased, the questions are not inferences. But they imply that an inference is possible. When one asks "Why did North Korea attack South Korea?" the suggestion is that there is a set of statements that, when examined, will provide a statement answering the original question. Such a set of statements is called an explanation and differs from the set of statements that one might use to predict that another world war will break out within five years. Explanations, like other kinds of inferences, attempt to interpret the world in ways that make it easier to grasp that world.

Patterns of inference

Statements made about the future, generalizations, and explanations represent situations in which man has attempted to arrange sets of statements into patterns that will allow him to derive conclusions that will be agreed on by others. Some of the patterns that have been developed to enable us to derive inferences are very old. The Greek philosophers talked about the classical syllogism, and it is a pattern still used today. Other patterns are newer or have been refined from earlier models. Any model or pattern developed, however, has been developed with a view toward two goals. These goals are **rigor** and **fidelity**. The rigor of a deductive analysis allows application of the same pattern to any set of data, always yielding the same inference. Fidelity of pattern means that any two people can apply a pattern to a set of data and obtain the same results.

The speech communicator is looking for inferential patterns that he can apply in that part of his preparation in which he looks for conclusions about which he might be confident. He might use those same patterns in transmitting the material to a set of auditors, but the complexity required of some patterns of inference may preclude his inclusion of the entire pattern in the actual speech. The question of developing a structural pattern that will serve as an adequate vehicle for speech presentation will be considered in Chapter 7, but this chapter's concern is with an analysis of the inferential process.

The following discussion will examine four different patterns or structures that have been commonly used to derive inferences. Some evidence suggests that these four patterns are not completely independent, that there are points of overlap, but each pattern seems complete enough to be considered separately. They are (1) The Deductive Pattern, (2) The Probabilistic Pattern, (3) The Functional Pattern, and (4) The Genetic Pattern.

The deductive pattern

The oldest of all forms of logic, the deductive pattern was first described in detail by Aristotle in his two works the **Prior Analytics** and the **Posterior Analytics.** The pattern probably has wider acceptance than any other model, and it is held up by the scientist as the ideal pattern for analyzing scientific problems. The simplest of all deductive forms is the **classical syllogism,** which serves to illustrate the deductive model in its oldest form.

Most people have run across the most famous syllogism:

> All men are mortal.
> Socrates was a man.
> Therefore, Socrates was mortal.

What does this pattern contain? First, it contains a very general premise: "All men are mortal." Then it contains a premise that relates a third event to the first two: "Socrates is a member of the class of men." And finally, it contains a conclusion, an inference, that links the remaining event to the second premise: "Socrates is then related to the class of mortals." This is the pattern for all deductions, no matter how complicated they become. Some general premises are stated, and specific conclusions are then inferred or deduced from the general premises.

Before proceeding further, the concept of **validity** must be introduced and defined. The communicator who is concerned with the development of patterns, or models, wants to be able to use those patterns in many different situations, with many different types of data. Such patterns should be independent of the physical world, patterns that would make it possible to derive conclusions from nonsense syllables if desired. When a pattern is internally consistent, and its parts "hang together," the argument is **valid.** Validity and the truth that comes from verification are independent. A conclusion may be true, yet derived from an argument that is not valid. For example, consider the following argument:

> All students are women.
> All women are basketball players.
> Therefore, all students are basketball players.

The conclusion is obviously false, but the argument is valid. It is internally consistent. Why should anyone be concerned with developing a tool that will enable him to make inferences that might be false? Because **if** one has a valid argument, and **if** he tests his two premises and finds that they are true, then he can be positive that the conclusion is also true, without further testing. The power of deduction lies in this fact. It enables us to derive new statements about the world from statements that have already been tested, and to **know** that the derived statements are also true if the logical structure used was adequate. Thus, the test for the deductive pattern is whether or not it is a valid pattern.

When Aristotle developed and amplified the ideas that Greek philosophers had about the **syllogism,** he did so on the basis of four general types of sentences. These are:

Type	*Structure*	*Example*
A	All A is B.	All Russians are Communists.
E	No A is B.	No Swedes are citizens of Japan.
I	Some A is B.	Some Americans are students.
O	Some A is not B.	Some women are not students.

The A and E sentence types are called **Universals,** whereas the I and O types are referred to as **Particulars.** The sentence types obviously fit many different situations. and any word representing an individual or a class of objects may be placed where A and B occur in the sentences.

To form a classical syllogism, one merely makes some combination of the sentences. The syllogism has three such sentences, such as AAA, or EIO, or AIO. Then one must examine the resulting structure to determine whether the last sentence in the structure, the conclusion, has been validly derived. But to do this, one needs a set of rules. Over the years, logicians have developed several such sets of rules. Each of them differs only slightly, and the one used below is the set discussed by Ambrose and Lazerowitz, as representative of many such sets.[1]

Before presenting a set of rules for determining the validity of a syllogism, the term **distribution** must be defined. Look at the A sentence type. Ask yourself whether you have looked at all the members of the class that is being discussed or only part of the class. In the sentence **All Russians are Communists,** you have had to look at "All Russians" in order to make the statement that they are "all Communists." Therefore, you may say that the term "Russians" is **distributed.** On the other hand, you do not have to look at all the Communists to make the statement. There might be many other members of the class Communist than those who are Russians. The term "Communist" is **not distributed.** In the E sentence type, both A and B are distributed. When one says that **No Swedes are citizens of Japan,** he must have looked at all "Swedes" and all "citizens of Japan." So both terms are distributed. In the I type, neither term is distributed. In the O type, the B term is distributed, but the A term is not.

A second word that must be defined is the **middle term.** Look at the arrangement:

All A is B.
All B is C.
Therefore, all A is C.

Here, the term B appears in both of the first two premises. This is called the **middle term.** If there is no middle term, there is no syllogism, and nothing can be inferred from the arrangement.

If one does have a set of three sentences, containing only three terms, and each sentence is of the A, E, I, or O type, one can determine the **validity of the conclusion** produced by applying the following rules to the structure:

1. The middle term must be distributed in at least one of the sentences.

2. No term undistributed in the premises may be distributed in the conclusion.

[1]Alice Ambrose and Morris Lazerowitz, **Fundamentals of Symbolic Logic** (New York: Rinehart, 1948), pp. 255–277.

3. If either of the first two premises are of the A or E type, the conclusion must be of the A or E type.

4. If both premises are negative, no conclusion can be drawn.

5. If one premise is negative, then the conclusion must be negative.

6. If neither premise is negative, the conclusion must be positive.

7. If both premises are particular, no conclusion can be drawn.

8. If the major premise is I and the minor premise is negative, no conclusion can be drawn.

This is the formal set of rules that can be applied to any syllogism in order to determine whether or not it is valid. Let us look at some examples, and apply the rules in order to see whether the syllogisms are valid.

1. All A is B.
   All C is B.
   All C is A.

This syllogism is invalid. Rule 1 applies, and the middle term (B) is not distributed in either premise.

2. All A is B.
   No C is A.
   No C is B.

This syllogism is invalid. Rule 2 applies, and the B term is not distributed in the first premise, but it is distributed in the conclusion.

3. No A is B.
   All A is C.
   Some C is not B.

Again, this syllogism is invalid. Rule 3 applies because this is a particular conclusion with universal premises.

The real value of the syllogism lies in its ability to analyze relationships between statements. If one has two premises that he has examined in some way, and knows to be true, he can make a syllogism in which the conclusion will also be true. However, although this is a very powerful tool, it does have limitations. For one thing, the classical syllogism is limited to expressions that fall within one of the four sentence types. Another serious limitation is that complicated situations are difficult to analyze using the classical syllogism. For example, consider the following argument:

The United States must always retaliate when its economic and political interests have been crossed. We know this because all countries
that have failed to retaliate in such circumstances have eventually
been overrun.

This argument can be restated in syllogistic form. To do so, the
logician has to decide what the terms are in the argument. Then he
has to decide what the premises are, and how they ought to be
arranged. When this is done, he is in a position to check the syllogism to see whether it is valid. And finally, he will have to find
some way of deciding whether or not the premises of the syllogism
are true, since if this determination cannot be made, then even if
the syllogism is valid, the conclusion may not be true.

Try your hand at putting the above argument into formal syllogistic form, and checking to see whether or not it is valid. It takes
time and is a difficult task. When the argument gets much more
complicated, even a highly trained logician would have trouble
putting the argument into syllogistic form.

More complicated messages can be handled by logical systems
other than the classical syllogistic model that has just been presented. Although there is not enough space to present some of these
models in detail, they need at least brief description. The most
general way of describing them is to say that they are **propositional
calculi.** Such advanced logical systems allow for the development of
ways of handling entire propositions containing such terms as "or,"
"and," "if ———, then ———," and "if ——— and only if ———, then ———."
The classical syllogism was developed for working with **classes** of
objects. The propositional calculus was developed to work with sets
of propositions.

Whether the communicator uses the syllogism or one of the
newer deductive models, his objectives are the same. He is interested in taking statements that have been accepted as evidence and
seeing what other standards can be derived from them. The use of
deduction in the analysis of speech materials should not be con-
fused with the presentation of materials in speeches. In the actual
presentation, the communicator may well choose to eliminate men-
tion of certain obvious premises, to state the conclusion without
any premises at all, or to reword the conclusion so that it will make
better semantic sense to the auditor. In fact, the auditor may never
know from the manner in which the speech is presented that the

conclusion actually was arrived at as the result of a deductive analysis.

In the speech itself, one expects to find such statements as "Democracy is the best system of government for the United States," "All juvenile delinquents ought to be taught how to behave by placing them in jail," "John Doe will be arrested soon, because he has been placed on the F.B.I.'s Most Wanted list," or "The typhoid breakout means that our community needs a new sewerage system." These and similar statements represent truncated syllogisms, syllogisms with one premise omitted. The technical term for arguments that appear in this shortened version is **enthymene,** and they represent one of the most important sources of speech materials. Such enthymenes have a deductive pattern in back of the statement as it is heard by the listener, and the speech communicator ought to be able to make a deductive analysis for his own information and for auditors who might question the statement without such an analysis.

Deduction is a powerful tool. With it, one can derive statements that are implied by some other statement. With it, one can determine the validity of many linguistic structures that he might be using. With it, he can establish the truth of statements without the necessity of making observations himself. It is one of the major ways in which the communicator can establish proof for an audience.

The probabilistic pattern

The preceding text mentioned, but did not emphasize, one of the major limitations of the deductive pattern. The communicator must be absolutely sure that the premises of the deductive argument are **true,** or he cannot say anything about the truth of the conclusion. Unfortunately, in most circumstances it is impossible to establish the truth of a premise with complete certainty. But when deduction uses a statement like "All doctors are competent," it assumes that the statement is completely, 100-per-cent true. It means that the statement has been checked out and the competence of every existing doctor has been determined. This is an obvious impossibility. The best any person could be expected to do is to say that that statement is **probably true** or **probably false.** The probabilistic pattern has been developed in order to examine the large class of statements that can be established as either true or false at a level of certainty less than 100 per cent.

At a very simple level, the probabilistic model is easy to examine. Imagine a group of forty people who belong to a club. Every year the club elects a new president. An investigator would like to find out ahead of time who the new president is likely to be. So he goes to each member of the club and asks for whom he intends to vote. If he finds that 24 out of the 40 people say that they intend to vote for Jones, he will conclude that Jones will be the next president of the club. Note that his conclusion, while stated as a fact, is only probably true. It could be that some people will change their minds before the vote actually takes place. It is possible that some people deliberately gave false answers to throw him off the track. It is possible that Jones would not accept the presidency. It is possible that the investigator did not count correctly. Other reasons might well intervene to make what was accepted as true turn out to be not true.

The club example is easy, because everyone in the group can be asked for his opinion. But let us imagine that one wishes to know who will be the next governor of Michigan. The state has approximately 4,000,000 residents who will be eligible to vote in the next election. The chances are that one can never ask each and every one of these people for whom he will vote. An investigator may say, "Well, with that many people, I won't need to ask them all, I'll just ask everyone that I can get what candidate he will vote for." If any significant number of voters are not asked, an accurate conclusion cannot be drawn. A conclusion will be drawn that will allow much variation. Suppose that as many as 50,000 of the 4,000,000 are asked. Suppose that 55 per cent say that they expect John Jones to win the election. Is 55 per cent the same figure that would be obtained if all 4,000,000 were questioned? If a different 50,000 people had been picked, would the same figure of 55 per cent have been obtained? Does the 55 percent mean that each one of those people will actually vote for Jones, or does it mean that 55 per cent think that Jones will win, even if they themselves do not intend to vote for him? Is there any way in which to be sure that the 55 per cent figure is not really going to be 49 per cent on election day?

These are probability questions, questions that ask how a limited number of cases can be examined and yet yield a statement that will be accurate about a much larger group of people or objects or events. Predictions about election results are only one type of probability question. A probability model must be used if one is interested in whether Russia will be willing to adhere to the terms of a new treaty, in how wide a highway must be for an anticipated load of cars, in the number of classrooms needed for a projected new elementary school, or in whether a safety feature for a new automobile will save enough lives to justify its cost. What are the characteristics of questions that must be answered by applying a probability model to the data?

First, the question must be one that attempts to draw some general conclusions from the examination of smaller bits of data. Suppose one wishes to establish that juvenile delinquents come from poor home environments. This would be his general conclusion. To establish this conclusion, he would have to look at the home environments of a great many individual juvenile delinquents. If he found that every juvenile delinquent he looked at had a poor home environment, then he would conclude that "All juvenile delinquents have poor home environments." Here he would be going from the specific to the general; this is one major characteristic of probability questions, or as they are sometimes called, **problems in induction.**

Second, the question must be one in which it is impossible to look at all cases. If one asks how many black marbles are in a set of twenty marbles lying on a table, he does not need to state his answer in probability terms. He would just count and report how many there are. But if there is a large jar filled with a mixture of black and white marbles, and someone hands him a handful of the marbles from the jar and wants to know how many black ones are in the entire jar, he has a probability problem. He must estimate on the basis of the sample drawn from the jar exactly how many black marbles are in the jar. Or, referring to the juvenile delinquents mentioned, it is very unlikely that **all** juvenile delinquents can be examined, because they are being created faster than they can be found. So the investigator has to estimate the home environment of juvenile delinquents from the sample of delinquents that he finally chooses to look at.

This second requirement needs further explication. When the communicator or scientist or analyst is faced with only a limited number of observations, or with some study that he can conduct only once, or with an event that can be observed by only a few people, general conclusions can be reached only in the form of a "bet" about what the true world, the real situation, is like. Given this kind of evidence, the communicator is always unsure about the correctness of any conclusion he might make about the true state of affairs. The probability model provides ways in which to assess this uncertainty and to calculate the probability that one will be wrong if he makes a given inference. When one has some idea of how wrong he is likely to be in a given situation, he is in a much better position to decide what he can say and do about the situation. For example, if he looks at a sample of juvenile delinquents and finds that 85 per cent come from poor home environments, he may decide that improvement of that environment will lead to a decrease in the number of such delinquents and act accordingly. He could be wrong in the analysis of the situation, but at least he would be operating on evidence that establishes the probable truth of the inference.

The third requirement for the application of a probability model to an inferential question is that the events concerned must be of such a nature that they can be **described.** This may seem to be a peculiar requirement, but it becomes less so when one realizes that the model to be built will be dependent largely on an underlying mathematical model. Such a mathematical model demands that the events to be quantified or numbered can be separated from other events that differ in any way. If there is absolutely no way of distinguishing between different events, no one will ever be able to draw inferences about the possibility of future occurrence of the events, or about the possibility that these events differ from other events.

The final requirement is that the events dealt with be **repeatable.** Inferences cannot be drawn about an event that is unique in time and space. Certainly, every event is unique in some respect, but this requirement suggests only that the events used be repeatable in principle. For example, if I throw a die on the table, and obtain a six, it is true that I cannot ever throw that same die in the same way, and at the same time. Time passes on, and one can never return to exactly the same spot in space and time. But the requirement is merely that I be able to throw the die again. This I can do; thus the event is repeatable.

Let us now assume that a given question fits all the requirements. **The probability that any event will occur can be defined as the proportion of the time that it will happen in the long run.** This definition of probability needs further explication. Assume that one is interested in determining whether some observation is really representative of the true state of affairs. How does he decide that it was not just a random chance happening, but rather represents the most likely thing to happen in similar circumstances? For example, if I were to shuffle a deck of cards, and ask you to draw a card, and you drew the deuce of hearts, would you then decide that you would draw the deuce of hearts every time I asked you to perform the same task? Most would not make this decision, nor bet any money at even odds on drawing the same card twice in succession. If the deck is an honest deck, and if the dealer shuffles the cards honestly, there are fifty-two cards in the deck, and the probability of any of them turning up on a single draw is 1/52. These are small odds. But the probability that the deuce of diamonds would be drawn twice in a row is 1/52 times 1/52 or a probability of 1/2,704. This possibility is so remote that few would bet on its happening. By chance alone, however, it could happen once in every 2,704 times the experiment is repeated.

How does one decide whether or not an inference can be made at a high-enough probability level to accord the inference the status of proof? The easiest answer is that he **cannot,** that these decisions can never be made with absolute certainty, and can thus never be said to be in a position to be used as proof. Harder to understand, but perhaps more helpful to the communicator, is the answer that although one can never be absolutely, 100-per-cent sure that his inferences are going to be correct, he can establish an area of agreement such that any inference established within it is one to be believed in and operated on. The scientist has several such areas. If he can say that the probability of an event occurring by chance is less than 1/20 or less than 1/100, he will usually say that he is willing to accept the inference as correct. Note, however, that he could be wrong. If an event could occur by chance 1 out of 100 times, it might well be that the time the investigator selected was the one time.

Let us look at the process. Imagine that a researcher wishes to determine whether a seven-year-old boy is more attracted to baseball equipment than to dolls. The probability pattern says that his first step is to deny that there is **any** relationship between the boy and the baseball or between the boy and the doll. In other words, he must hypothesize that the boy will choose equally between the ball and the doll when he is given an equal opportunity to choose either one. Such a hypothesis is called a "null hypothesis" and is the initial guess that there is no relationship between the two events one is concerned with, i.e., that the boy will choose the ball as many times as he chooses the doll.

Now the investigator sets up a situation. He places the ball and the doll in cabinets and tells the boy to go to a cabinet and choose either the baseball or the doll. The boy chooses the ball. If either event is as likely to occur as the other, the probability of his choosing the ball is 1/2. No one would conclude from this evidence that the hypothesis of no difference should be rejected, because it could be argued that not enough cases have been examined. He repeats the study, and again the boy selects the ball. He does the experiment for a third time, and again the boy picks the ball. Now can the investigator conclude by saying that he has proved that this seven-year-old boy will choose the baseball over the doll? To make this decision, he first needs to enumerate what outcomes are possible. If he uses B for a choice of the ball, and D for the choice of the doll, there are eight possible arrangements of choices that could have been made.

BBB	BDD
BBD	DBD
BDB	DDB
DBB	DDD

Each one of these eight possible events is equally likely to occur. The boy chose the ball three straight times. This is the event BBB. If the choice was determined merely by chance, the event BBB had a 1/8 chance of being chosen. Or another way of saying it, is to say that the probability of observing an event as likely as BBB is 1/8. If the experiment was repeated eight more times, another BBB situation could be expected to occur, by chance alone, at least once. One might be willing to conclude that a probability of 1/8 is good enough to say that he has "proved" that boys prefer baseballs to dolls, but most scientists would not make such a conclusion on that evidence. They would like to be even more certain that they are correct in rejecting the null hypothesis and arguing for the alternative hypothesis that boys prefer balls. In the social sciences, a probability level of 1/20 is usually considered to be the minimum level of acceptability, and many scientists would not be willing to make conclusions until they had seen results at a 1/100 level. In the case used as an example, a pattern of BBBBB would be necessary to reach a probability level of less than 1/20, and the boy would have to choose at least seven times in order to reach a level better than 1/100.

Even if the boy made his choice ten times in a row, and each time he chose the ball over the doll, one would not be able to say with complete certainty that boys prefer balls to dolls, because, even then, there is a probability of 1/1,024 of having the ten-times-in-a-row choice occur by chance alone. But for most of us, and for most scientists, that would be enough evidence to enable us to infer that the null hypothesis is wrong, and that some alternative hypothesis must be selected. The probability pattern does not allow direct support of the hypothesis that the boy prefers baseballs to dolls. Rather answers must be obtained in an indirect manner.

Using the probabilistic pattern is an indirect manner of obtaining proof for the public speaker. The method never says that conclusions are correct. It says only that the opposites of the conclusions have a high probability of being incorrect. The decision as to when an inference has been "proved" to be correct is an arbitrary one. For one person, three broken windows in a period of three months is enough evidence for him to decide that somebody was deliberately "out to get him." For another person, the same three broken panes of glass represent only a series of accidents, a "rare" event, but not a deliberate plot. Can a communicator ever be sure? No, he can become more and more positive, he can show more and more conclusively that his inference is likely to be the best one, but he can never be sure that what happened did not occur by chance rather than by design.

Another example will show how people may react to probabilities. This incident occurred when the author was just beginning college. I had been hired to sell soda pop during the Illinois State Fair and found myself working with a group of men who traveled from fair to fair all summer long. At night, after the day's work was done, and the soda "butchers" had received their pay for the day, they retired to a small room under the stands to change clothes. Invariably, a card game or a dice game would be started, and after a long hot day, there was frequently a great deal of money in the game. One evening, when the money was piling up, an incident took place that indicated just how arbitrary our decisions are about probabilities. The man with the dice had just thrown his fifth "7" and was about to throw for the sixth time. Just then, one of the bettors reached over and quietly laid an open razor on top of the pile of money. The shooter looked at the razor, looked at the dice, threw, and lost. He picked up what money he had not lost on the throw and left the room and the fair. Were the dice honest? I will never know. It is certainly possible to throw five 7's in a row, but the probability of that event occurring by chance is low. So low that the man with the razor decided that he could no longer support the null hypothesis that says that the dice are honest. He chose to support an alternative hypothesis—either the dice or the shooter were dishonest. He was operating on probabilities. The same problem faces any communicator who must accept and operate on inferences that must be established by using the probability pattern.

The steps to the probability pattern for assessing inferences include:

1. Determine what events are involved in the situation. How many different outcomes are there for these events? Determine on the basis of a chance estimate what the probability of occurrence of each event is. In the examples used, the probability of any one event has been assumed to be equal to the probability for any other event. In some situations, this is not the case.

2. Determine what the null hypothesis is. With three different events, it may be hypothesized that the probability of event A is equal to the probability of event B is equal to the probability of event C ($Pr\ A = Pr\ B = Pr\ C$). Remember that the null hypothesis is based on an assumption that these events occur by chance alone.

3. Determine what level of confidence is acceptable. If the results obtained could not occur by chance alone as much as 5 per cent of the time, is this satisfactory? Or is a 1/10 level—or a 1/100 level—better? The level set is up to the communicator but some level must be set or no conclusions can be drawn.

4. Make the observations needed. These can be drawn from historical examples, be actual observations made about a group of people or ideas or events, or be observations made in the laboratory. Enough observations must be made to assure that the probability of occurrence can be computed so that the null hypothesis can be rejected if it is wrong. Observations should be collected at random, so that any observation has as much chance of occurring as any other observation.

5. Determine how likely it is that the sequence of events observed could have happened by chance alone. This step should result in some fraction or decimal ranging from 0 to 1.00. One can never have a probability larger than 1, nor smaller than 0.

6. Compare the figure obtained with the level of confidence set in step 3. Suppose that the probability of occurrence of the sequence of events observed is 1/10, given that the events occurred by chance alone. Suppose that the level of confidence desired was 1/20. The obtained probability is larger than the level of confidence; the null hypothesis cannot be rejected, and the case has not been proved. On the other hand, suppose that the obtained probability figure was 1/30. This probability value is smaller than the level of confidence set up, and the null hypothesis can be rejected; one can then say that the chances are that the inference is correct. The case will have been proved.

This is the probability model. As it is described, it sounds completely different from the deductive model. It is really related quite closely to the deductive model, and the relationship shows that the deductive model cannot produce conclusions that are completely certain. The preceding discussion of the deductive model pointed out that one can be sure that the conclusion is true if the premises are true, and if the syllogism is valid. But it did not ask how one established the truth of the premises. The discussion of induction and the use of the probability pattern suggests that one might use induction to establish the truth of the premises that he uses in a syllogism. Take the following syllogism, which is valid:

All animals have two kidneys.
All men are animals.
All men have two kidneys.

In this deductive argument, it has to be established that all animals have two kidneys. But it is impossible to look at all animals. So one must turn to induction and establish that it is very probable that all animals have kidneys. Because it cannot be established "beyond the shadow of a doubt" that all animals have kidneys, and one can only say that it is very probable that all animals have kidneys, the conclusion that all men have two kidneys cannot be drawn with complete confidence either. Thus, regardless of whether the communicator uses induction and a probability model or a deductive model to establish inferential proof, his inferences can never be completely guaranteed.

An inference based on a probability model is a statement made about the world from a sample drawn from that world. Such an inference is no better than the results of the sample drawn. It is generalization, based on an examination of a portion of the events. Such generalizations play an important part in speech-making and in the decisions that lead an individual to become a communicator.

The functional pattern

In many areas of concern to the communicator, proof takes the form of indicating one or more functions that an event plays in determining the way in which an entire system operates. Such proofs may also be termed "teleological" explanations or proofs. Philosophers raise a number of objections to the use of functional explanations as proof, and these undoubtedly limit the kinds of situations and questions to which this type of pattern may apply. Nevertheless, functional explanations are accepted as proof by auditors and are used by communicators to make decisions. An understanding of functional explanations would thus seem important to the communicator.

During most of the 1960's, the United States has been concerned with the "New Frontier" of the late President Kennedy or with the "Great Society" of President Johnson. The central issue signaled by these phrases is the nature and quality of American life. What can we do about poverty? What will a dependence on computers do for the lives of people in the United States? How about the problem of the high school drop-out? Will birth control help improve the quality of American life? These and similar questions form the core of current controversies. It is difficult to "prove" that the country needs any of the programs that have been offered in the Congress. Induction would help a little in providing statistics about the extent of any of the problems. Deduction would be helpful, except that the major premises on which deduction must rest have not been established.

What has happened is that debaters on both sides have used the functional pattern in order to establish the soundness of their positions. Those who are in favor of federal aid for schools, railroads, and so forth, have attempted to explain the role that schools, railroads, or airlines play in the society and to indicate the necessity that such institutions be preserved. The logical conclusion for this side of the question is that the federal government has the duty and the right to aid in the attempt to preserve such institutions, or the moral duty, in the case of the poor, to aid in trying to remove the problem of poverty from society. Opposition speakers have also used a functional explanation. They have looked at the role of the federal government and the role of the states and local agencies. They point out that it costs more when the federal government undertakes such efforts, that it is not the role that the federal government should take, and that these problems have been with us for years. They feel that there is no evidence that these problems are not an integral part of the structure of our society.

Let us consider one of the arguments from the "Great Society" debates as further illustration of the functional pattern. President Johnson introduced the term "A War on Poverty" early in his administration. The debates in Congress resulted in a package of bills and an appropriation of money to carry out the program. The debates centered around a whole complex of smaller issues, and almost all of them were presented as arguments derived from a functional pattern. The proponents of President Johnson's program argued that the structure of our society was not such that the poor were an integral part of it. They argued that the role of the poor in our society was such as to drag down living conditions for the rest of society. They argued that if poverty could be eliminated, the entire society would reach heights never before attained.

The opponents argued that there has never been a society without its poor, that they are not created by others but rather that they create themselves. They suggested that even if money were poured into the economy in an attempt to raise living standards for the poverty-stricken that eventually this money would again wind up in the hands of those who are not poor. In other words, they argued that the way in which the society functions is such that the poor are an integral part of that structure, and that attempts made to overcome a part of the basic structure of the society would destroy it.

Without discussing the "rightness" of either position, let us consider the nature of the arguments used. On both sides, the arguments were functional—were attempts to establish the desirability or reasons for a claim by showing how the claim was related to some larger structure. A scientist would use a functional explanation to explain the liver, showing what functions the liver plays in the operation of the body. The conservationist wishing to preserve a species from extinction would attempt to show the role that the species plays in maintaining the balance of nature and the probable results to be expected from attempts to extinguish it. The college president wanting to show that the student body should be composed of students from all over the United States rather than from a single state or locality would attempt to show the role played by such students in broadening the education received by the majority of students in the school. The social scientist justifies his very existence, in part, by using functional analyses. He uses them to ascertain how social systems—e.g., the United States—perpetuate themselves by maintaining their structure and to demonstrate that changes in the social system are also likely to be accompanied by changes in the social structure.

How does one make a functional analysis? Three steps make up the process. First, identify the whole structure to be examined. It might be the school system in a particular town or the city governmental structure. It could be a structure as large as the "society of the United States" or as small as "the governing organization of my church." The larger structure must be identified as carefully as possible, or the analysis will be made on elements that do not really play a part in the larger structure.

Second, identify the elements of the larger structure. This is not always as easy as it may seem. Any structure may be analyzed at different levels, but the communicator is usually interested in a particular level of analysis for any given question. If the school system is the larger structure, individual schools within the system may be used as the unit of analysis, or classrooms within the system, or grades in the entire system, or principals, or teachers, or even individual students. If the interest lies in raising individual teacher's pay, an analysis based on classrooms as the smaller unit might be inappropriate. In making the selection of the unit of analysis to be used for any larger structure, the ultimate purpose of the analysis must be considered.

Third, determine the role played by each of the units of analysis in the larger structure. This means more than merely indicating the immediate function played by some element within the total structure. It usually means that the analyst must also determine, if possible, what changes can be expected in the larger structure if changes are made for any element within it. This then means that the analyst must determine what **values** each element can take and what changes in those values will mean to the structure as a whole. To use the school system again, take the teacher as the unit of analysis, and ask what will happen to the school system as a whole if one group of teachers is treated differently from another group of teachers. If salaries for the science teachers are raised, what effect will this have on other teachers? If new classroom facilities are provided for the high-school teachers in the system, what are the probable effects on the rest of the teachers in the system? This third step, therefore, is a crucial one, explaining not only the immediately observable function of the elements in any system, but also explaining how changes in those elements can be expected to affect the system as a whole.

Once an analysis has been made, the communicator will use the results to make decisions regarding his initial question. Decisions cannot be so precise with a functional analysis as with a deductive model or a probabilistic pattern. But when the communicator must make decisions affecting the structure of some social organization, and when an analysis of that structure in terms of the function played by elements within the structure will assist in explaining the nature of the structure, a functional analysis is extremely useful.

Once he has made a decision, the communicator will have the task of communicating it to an auditor or set of auditors. Here, the functional pattern is of extreme utility. Many audiences are not able to follow a deductive analysis of the situation. In fact, as will be discussed in Chapter 7, even well-educated groups are not able to follow deductive analyses very well. The same can be said for complicated probabilistic patterns of analysis. Statistics quickly get complicated, and the average listener will have trouble following what is being done and being referred to in any situation. The functional analysis does not seem to have these limitations. In presenting materials to an audience, the communicator will find it very useful to structure his arguments, and perhaps even his entire speech, in the form of a functional analysis. The analysis can be simplified greatly, while still retaining the shape and form of the functional pattern. This is indeed an analytic and communication tool that should be in the "toolbox" of every communicator.

The genetic pattern

Philosophers disagree on whether the genetic pattern of inference is a distinct type of inference, or only a subclass of probabilistic patterns. The characteristics of the genetic pattern are distinctive, however, and the pattern tends to be used frequently in questions of public policy. It seems reasonable to present it as a distinctive type of inferential proof, and let concern over its classification be left to the philosopher.

The genetic pattern sets out the sequence of major events through which one system changes and matures into some present system. In this sense, therefore, the pattern could be called a historical pattern. It looks over the entire pattern of past events that seem to be connected with some present event and tries to suggest which of the past events contributes most to the present state of affairs. By abstracting the characteristics of the events thus isolated, the analyst can attempt to predict the future direction of the system.

Assume that one wishes to ask what will happen if the Congress of the United States passes a bill severely limiting the availability of firearms to the American public. An opponent of such legislation might use the genetic pattern to attempt to defeat the bill. He would cite the instances of Germany, Japan, and other countries that severely limited the rights of the people to own firearms before World War II and suggest that it was this restriction on citizens' liberty that led to the later formation of totalitarian governments. Then he might turn to some of the Scandinavian countries that also limit firearm use and point out that it was this restriction that made it easy for the Germans to overrun these countries in the same war. In other words, he would pick out major events in history, in an attempt to show that the best prediction one can make of the future is on the basis of the past, and emphasize that the predicted event or action is not what the United States needs.

A proponent of such legislation may also use a genetic approach. He might point to the rising rate of crime in the United States and to the number of people shot with firearms purchased under uncontrolled conditions. He might also single out World War II, but use it for another point. He might show that much of the equipment left over from the Second World War has found its way legally into the hands of criminals. He would then suggest that such legislation does not destroy the rights of potential buyers, but merely attempts to protect the rights of others.

A real argument from a genetic pattern is one familiar to all college debaters. This is the argument that the United States is much like Great Britain. A debater shows the points of similarity between the two systems and concludes that the two systems are essentially comparable. Then he goes on to show that Great Britain adopted some policy in the past, such as socialized medicine, and the result has been present advantages for the English people. He continues his argument to suggest that if the United States were to adopt socialized medicine, the country would obtain the same advantages for its people.

The genetic pattern falls into three steps. First, describe the system to be investigated. The same cautions raised about the functional pattern can be raised about the genetic pattern. The system must be described precisely, and the level at which analysis is to take place must be described in some detail.

Second, describe the sequence of major events through which the present system came to be. This is obviously the most difficult step, leading to the kind of controversy that is frequent about control of firearms, school education, or water conservation. Which events are the "major" ones? Which events should be ignored as unimportant in the development of an idea or system? The analyst must have a set of assumptions upon which he chooses those events that should be considered in the analysis. They may be assumptions suggesting that economic events are more important than political events, that events involving leaders of a state or country are more important than events involving ordinary people, or that scientific developments are more likely to lead to changes in the system than developments in literature. There is no way to determine absolutely which assumptions are better, but the communicator must select the past events of the system he is describing on **some** basis.

Third, describe the causal chain that leads from the events selected to the present state of the system. Again, this is not easy. Causality can never be absolutely determined. Look at such a simple event as a rainfall. What caused the rain to fall? Was it the presence of clouds bearing water; or was it the drop in temperature, causing the water to condense; or was it the passage of the cloud through a dust cloud? For any given rainstorm, it might be one of these events, or two, or, most probably, a combination of all three. But the causality cannot be determined with perfect confidence. Even when a high correlation between two events can be shown, causality can be implied, but it can never be established with certainty. In spite of the impossibility of establishing causality with absolute certainty, the genetic pattern demands that the analyst try to show the causal links between the events he has shown as important and the system he is describing.

These are the steps that set up the genetic pattern. Once it is set up, the communicator can make decisions about his initial question. He might decide that firearms control will be unwise, or that public education needs to have more governmental support, or that the police need more authority. His decision will be based on a genetic analysis.

The major objection to the genetic pattern has already been suggested, but it needs to be made more explicitly. Not every event in the previous history of a social system will be selected for consideration as important to the present. But when two people view the system, the chances are very good that they will select different events as important. The selection of different events may well lead to different conclusions regarding questions of public policy. Because all such selections of events are to some extent arbitrary, one cannot be positive that he has selected the most meaningful events. This is a severe limitation on the historical explanation, necessitating that the communicator look to other patterns of analysis before he decides that the genetic pattern is his best choice.

In spite of the severe limitations of the genetic pattern, its persuasive abilities are very high. Many audiences will have great respect for the communicator who argues from history, who appeals to events in the past as illustrative of decisions to be made at the present time. For example, the decision of the United States to pursue the war in Viet Nam further was presented to Americans as an argument from history. It was argued that a careful consideration of previous instances of a nation faced with aggression yields the conviction that the best results were obtained when aggression was met firmly, rather than when loopholes were left to the agressor nation. Such an argument has proven effective again and again, quite apart from its actual probative value.

Summary

This chapter has discussed the problem of inferences, statements made as the result of considering a structure built up from various pieces of evidence. Four patterns were discussed in detail: the deductive pattern, the probabilistic pattern, the functional pattern, and the genetic pattern.

Each of the patterns was discussed as a tool for analysis of questions in the public-policy area. It was suggested that the deductive pattern and the probabilistic pattern had the most value as tools for the analysis of inferential statements. It was also suggested that the functional pattern and the genetic pattern have perhaps less analytic rigor, but that they are important to the communicator because of their persuasive value in attempting to communicate a decision to an auditor or group of auditors.

SIX

Motivational proof: judgments

The nature of judgments

In **Gulliver's Travels**, Jonathan Swift makes an artistic controversy the basis for a war. Over the merits of opening eggs at the big end or at the little end, the little people of Lilliput embroil themselves in a bitter civil war. One can imagine orators from Lilliput rousing the people to patriotic heights by claiming that: "Teaching children to open eggs from the small end will lead to juvenile delinquency," or "It is a breach of public morals to open eggs from the large end." The egg argument sounds silly, but it capsulizes the problem of the relation between judgmental statements and proof.

When proof is defined as the process of using evidence to secure belief, judgments seem to be ruled out as a source of proof. Judgments **do** form a kind of evidence, however, and their use in speech communication **does** lead to changes in belief. Judgments must be considered, along with observations and inferences, as a primary source of the materials that the speaker will use to secure belief in his ideas.

In order to understand how the term "judgment" is used in this book, some understanding of the differences between observations and judgments is necessary. Listed below are four sentences that are clearly observations and four sentences that are clearly judgments:

Observations:

Gone with the Wind is one of the top ten money-makers of all time.

The Statue of Liberty was erected in 1876.

A positive relationship exists between smoking and lung cancer.

The Rembrandt painting "Aristotle Contemplating the Bust of Homer" recently sold for the highest price ever recorded in art history.

Judgments:

Gone with the Wind was the finest movie ever made.

The Statue of Liberty is the true symbol of the United States.

Smoking is a dirty, filthy habit.

The Rembrandt painting "Aristotle Contemplating the Bust of Homer" is undoubtedly the finest example of the master's work.

See the differences between the two sets of sentences. In the first four sentences, some way in which to check the truth of the statement can be set up. Old documents will give the date when the Statue of Liberty was erected. A list showing how much money was made by various films can be examined, disclosing whether **Gone with the Wind** was in the top ten. Any observation is capable of being verified in some fashion, even though it may be difficult or prohibitively expensive to do so.

The second four sentences, however, cannot be handled in the same fashion as the first four. There are no old records to indicate whether the Statue of Liberty is the "true symbol" of the United States. There is no way of ascertaining by a perusal of records whether the movie was the "finest" ever made. Not one of the second set of sentences can be verified. Checking with the physical world will never produce an answer regarding the truth of a judgmental statement. The only checking that can be done is with the maker of the statement. He can be asked whether he believes that smoking is a dirty, filthy habit. If he says yes, it has not been verified that the statement is true, but merely that someone believes that it is true.

The essential difference between an observation and a judgment lies in whether it can be verified. But the question of verification is dependent upon the relationship of the words used in the statement to physical reality. Observations stress the use of words that refer to physical reality, whereas judgments stress words that refer to personal or social reality. This distinction marks a difference in the kinds of meaning that are stressed in sentences of the two types and deserves further exploration.

Many words have their primary reference to an object or an activity that can be identified by anyone. These words carry a **denotative** meaning as their primary component. Such words as "erect," "sold," "smoking," "money," "husband," or "glass" are words that have as their primary meaning some agreed-upon relationship with an object or activity in the physical world. On the other hand, many other words do not have a primary relationship to the physical world. Their referent is to some cognitive state within an individual. Words in this category have a primarily **connotative** meaning. Such words as "finest," "beauty," "dramatic," "prejudiced," and "dirty" are words that carry a connotative meaning. There is no single place one can go to identify the meaning of words like these, except to the user of the word. "Dirty" covers an entirely different range of phenomena for the mother than for the three-year-old boy. What is a beautiful woman to one man may not be to the man sitting next to him. These words are largely evaluative in nature and reflect man's eagerness to place values on the objects he encounters and the ideas he has.

Words cannot be divided into two piles, one of words carrying a denotative meaning and another of words carrying a connotative meaning. All words have both a denotative-meaning component and a connotative-meaning component. The word "Russian" carries with it a meaning of "citizens of the Soviet Union." This is a denotative meaning. But "Russian" to many people also represents a "bad" or "untrustworthy" individual. This is a connotative meaning. The word "snake" carries a common denotative meaning to everyone. None of us would have much trouble identifying a "snake" if we were to see one. But connotative meanings for the term range all the way from a feeling of favorableness to feelings of abject horror and revulsion.

Even though all words carry both a connotative and a denotative component, usually one aspect rather than the other is emphasized. Thus, for most of us, the word "table" carries a largely denotative meaning. The word "beauty" carries primarily a connotative meaning. When words are used in statements, the statement is classified according to the nature of the words within the statement. Thus, a statement that uses words having primarily denotative meanings is what has been referred to as an observation. A statement that utilizes words carrying connotative meanings is a judgment. Words that are fairly equally split between denotative and connotative meanings make statements that are difficult to classify as either observations or judgments. The best the communicator can do is to make some attempt to identify the intent of the person making the statement. Was he intending to make an evaluation or an observation?

Generally, in communication, words that carry largely denotative meanings do not give the communicator the same kinds of problems as do words that carry largely connotative meanings. The reason for the differences in the ease the communicator can expect in handling situations lies in the way in which words are learned. Within a common culture, the basic vocabulary is learned in the same way by everyone. Every child learns to associate the word "dog" with the same class of objects. We have all learned, through the same process, equivalent denotative meanings for such words as "television," "toadstool," "fish," "education," and "mother." Thus, people who speak English will have a large group of words that they can use with the expectation that equivalent denotative meanings will be recognized by English-speaking auditors.

Even on the denotative level, however, there are words that will have several different meanings and objects for which several different words will be used by different subgroups within the culture. For example, look at the word "school." One could use it to refer to the formal education system, to a specific place in the city, to a group of fish, to the process of learning, and perhaps to other kinds of activities. Only the context will reveal what the term is being used for. The same object can be referred to by many different names. For example, "bream," "sunnies," "punkinseeds," and "gills" are among some of the names applied in different areas to common sunfish. On the denotative level, the speech communicator must make sure that his auditors will have the same meanings as he does for the terms he uses in his statements. However, his task is easier because common meanings are held by large segments of the population.

On the connotative level, however, the problem is quite different, and this forms the basic problem of this chapter. Connotative meanings are **not** the same for large segments of the population. Even when a group of auditors would tend to evaluate the same statement in the same way, the communicator would not know this and would have few ways of finding out that an audience has a common connotative meaning for a term. It is important to try to establish the kinds of connotative meanings held by individuals, for, if a group holds common meanings for a set of terms, those terms can be used in judgmental statements, and they will be treated as if they were observations. In order to establish a basis for predicting the ways in which judgments will be received by an auditor, let us consider: (1) the observations that lie behind every judgment; (2) the factors that influence the selection of judgments to be used in proof; and (3) the presentation of judgments as motivational proof.

The observation and the judgment

It has already been suggested that the judgment is a statement that emphasizes connotative meanings. Connotative meanings are personal to individuals and thus differ widely among individuals. However, connotative meanings, like denotative meanings, are learned through experiences with the world around us. The speech communicator can use the judgment as material to induce proof because judgments depend for their formation on a prior series of observations.

Look at a simple judgment, and go through the steps that an individual might have gone through before he came to believe in it. Take the statement, "Harvard is the best university in the United States." What observations might lie behind an individual's willingness to believe in and make that statement? He might have observed some of the graduates of Harvard, noting that, over the years, they achieved positions of prominence in government and industry. He might have observed the number of graduates going on to graduate school. He might have noted the amount of money given to Harvard in endowments, or the number of research grants made to the university, or the number of Nobel and Pulitzer prize winners teaching there. Or the individual could have read a series of statements, made by people he trusted, asserting that Harvard was the best university in the United States; trusting these sources, he became willing to make the same judgments. Presumably, if one looked far enough, he could find a series of observations that were made by someone, who arrived at a judgment after making the observations.

All judgments are made on some basis, and the speech communicator must locate the observations on which a judgment is based before he will understand the maker of the judgment, or before he can be completely willing to accept the judgment as proof. The problem is that some judgments are made on the basis of personal observation of a series of underlying events, and others are made after consideration of another series of judgments. To illustrate the latter situation, take the statement, "Sophia Loren is the world's most exciting woman." Such a statement is likely to be accepted as fact, and could be used in proof situations, by many persons. What are the observations behind the belief? For many who would say that they believe in the statement, the basis for the belief lies in their having read in a newspaper, or a movie magazine, that "Sophia Loren is the world's most exciting woman." Thus, the only observation the individual would have made before coming to this particular belief is to have read the statement in some magazine or heard it from a friend. Somewhere, at some time, someone must have made a series of observations that led him to make the statement, but the speech communicator is likely to find it impossible to ferret out the original evidence on which the statement is based.

Statements such as "Harvard is the best university in the United States" or "Sophia Loren is the world's most exciting woman" are judgments that are held at a **peripheral** level in the belief system of most individuals. Beliefs held at a peripheral level are likely to change drastically over a span of time and across subgroups in the culture. Look at conceptions of beauty over the years. The teenager of 1965 finds it impossible to understand why his grandparents considered Mary Pickford beautiful, and almost as impossible to understand why his parents thought Jean Harlow beautiful. Standards of clothing change from year to year. Musical tastes change. Preferences in political oratory change easily. Senator Everett M. Dirksen of Illinois has been pointed to as the last of a dying breed, but the reason the breed is dying is that tastes in oratory have changed so that speakers with a style similar to Dirksen's are not elected.

Some beliefs are held more strongly and change only slowly over the years. In 1965 the first "Medicare Bill" was passed in the

United States. Yet the idea was first suggested by President Harry S. Truman in 1945, when it met with ridicule and general opposition; and the idea had been debated in one form or another in the United States since the 1920's and in Europe since 1850. The values placed on government-sponsored medical care, and the observations that were made about such a program, changed only slowly over the years; but they did change. Individuals very seldom change their political-party affiliation, but the natures of the propositions that form the party platforms do change. The Democratic party has recently supported propositions that formed planks in the Socialist party platform of thirty years ago. The Republican party today is not the Republican party of Lincoln's time, or even of Coolidge's era. Judgments made about Medicare or about party platforms are also judgments made about authorities. As such, they form part of the **intermediate** level in the individual's belief structure. They may be held no more intensely than beliefs at a peripheral level, but they will be harder for the average auditor to change.

Finally, judgments may be made in reference to very strongly held beliefs—beliefs about religion, about life, about people, and about an individual's self-concept. When an individual has made a judgment that "All Negroes are lazy," or that "Man could not have descended from the apes," or "All juvenile delinquents come from poor home environments," he will tend to treat the judgments as factual statements. He will probably be very reluctant to change beliefs regarding such judgments, which lie in those areas previously defined as the **central** level in the individual's belief structure.

As suggested previously, the speech communicator has two tasks. He must formulate and establish the statements or the ideas he believes in; and he must then find ways of effectively communicating those ideas to others. From the discussion so far, a few more suggestions seem appropriate:

1. The speech communicator ought to ascertain the basis on which he makes the judgments he intends to communicate to others. Sometimes, such an analysis will lead him to change the judgment, or at least to search for more specific evidence.

2. The communicator ought to attempt to ascertain whether other individuals have made the same basic background observations as he has. If not, he must supply the auditor with such data before he can hope to have the auditor arrive at the same judgments.

3. The communicator must realize that a judgment in which the audience is likely to believe will have the same status as an observation. If one has made a series of observations and is willing to make the judgment that **"Gone with the Wind** was the finest movie ever made,"** he will treat that statement in exactly the same way as he treats the statement "The Washington Monument is in Washington, D. C." Thus, when the communicator is fashioning an argument in order to induce belief in an idea, he may be able to use judgments and have them treated as observations.

4. The communicator must note that judgments are likely to be placed by the auditor into various levels of his own belief structure and to be accepted or rejected according to the centrality of the judgment being presented. A judgment that "goes against" a central belief is likely to lead the auditor to reject the entire argument. On the other hand, a judgment that is in line with the individual's belief structure is likely to bring him to accept an idea even when there is little direct evidence to support it.

The selection of judgments for proof

For many observations, an individual can establish the truth of the observation by personal inspection of the events to which it corresponds. For some observations, and all judgments, this kind of personal inspection is impossible. The average American cannot go himself to Viet Nam, or Korea, or India to check the truth of statements made about the country. He must rely on the observations of others and a reporting system to get those observations to him. Judgments lie entirely in the minds of others, and we must depend on others to convey those judgments to us. But people who make judgments, and people who make observations, differ in their perceived ability as reporters or critics. One is inclined to trust the judgments of some and reject the judgments of others. When the same statement is made by two different people, and some auditors accept the statement from one communicator and reject it from the other, it can be said that either the credibility of the two sources is different or that different characteristics in the listeners lead them to different decisions.

Source credibility is a phenomenon pointed to by Aristotle when he talked about the **ethos** of certain speakers. The phenomenon is more easily understood in terms of experiments that show differences in belief or attitude change caused solely by the credibility of the speaker. One such experiment was first made by Haiman, and it has been repeated a number of times. Take a tape-recorded message that advocates socialized medicine. Then get a number of people, and divide them randomly into two groups. Ascertain by means of an attitude test what attitudes are held toward socialized medicine by members of both groups. For Group A, play the tape, and tell the members that the speech was made by a "sophomore at Northwestern University." For Group B, play the tape, and tell them that the speech was made by "the Surgeon General of the United States." Then measure the attitudes of both groups again, and determine how much attitude change there was for the groups. The investigator should find, as did Haiman,[1] that more members of Group B than of Group A changed to favor socialized medicine. Because the same tape was used for both groups, one must conclude that the differences in amount of attitude shift were a result of the influence of the source. The Surgeon General has more **source credibility** than does the sophomore.

For every individual, the sources from which he obtains information are arranged in a kind of hierarchy, with the most credible sources at the top and the least credible at the bottom. Thus, for one individual, the New York **Times** might be the most credible source, and for another, the minister of his church. For one individual, the president of the AFL-CIO might be the least credible source, and for another, the president of the United States Chamber of Commerce. Credibility varies with the topic under consideration. The President of the United States might be the most credible source when the topic is foreign policy, but the county agricultural agent might be more credible when the topic is hybrid seed corn.

Every source has a certain degree of credibility and will occupy a certain place within one's personal hierarchy of credible sources. But source credibility is not a unitary characteristic. Within it are at least three dimensions, or characteristics, perceived by the auditor as possessed by the communicator. According to the communicator's degree of possession of these three characteristics, an auditor will tend to place more or less faith in his message. The three

[1] F. S. Haiman, "An Experimental Study of the Effects of Ethos in Public Speaking," **Speech Monographs**, 2 (1949), 190–202.

dimensions, are recently described by Berlo, Lemert and Mertz,[2] are **trustworthiness, qualification** and **dynamism.** Trustworthiness comprises the general faith placed in an individual because of the position he holds or the record he has established for veracity over time. An individual who is perceived as trustworthy may speak on topics on which he is not an expert and be believed. Qualification is specific competence in a certain topic and seems to be a less general trait than trustworthiness. An individual may be considered an expert on one topic and not on another; he will be believed on the first topic and not necessarily believed on the other. Dynamism is a different sort of characteristic from either of the others. Some communicators are judged by auditors to be more dynamic than other communicators. Given two people, who are perceived to have the same level of trustworthiness and qualification on a topic, the individual who is perceived to be the more dynamic of the two will tend to have the more credibility. Dynamism is related to rate of speaking, amount of bodily action, tone, and perhaps other characteristics that are difficult to describe. President John F. Kennedy, for example, was perceived to be a dynamic speaker and was rated as more dynamic than President Dwight D. Eisenhower, though he was not necessarily more credible.

These three dimensions seem to be relatively independent of one another, although any speaker will be seen as possessing varying degrees of all three characteristics. The independence of the dimensions is indicated in such statements as "I don't think he knows much about the subject, but I don't think he would tell a lie," or "I don't trust him very much, but I love to listen to him talk," or "It is too bad that he can't get his ideas across, because he certainly knows what he is talking about." It is certainly possible for an individual to be perceived as trustworthy, qualified, and dynamic. The late President Kennedy was perceived in this fashion by many people, as are many other public figures.

Source credibility is stressed when talking about judgments because the auditor cannot check out the truth of a judgment against reality. The best he can do is to check out the maker of the judgment and decide whether he will believe that the individual is credible or not. Thus, the communicator can utilize source credibility in

[2]David K. Berlo, James B. Lemert, and Robert J. Mertz, **Evaluations of the Message Source: A Basis for Predicting Communication Effects,** Research Monograph, Department of Communication, Michigan State University, 1965.

two ways. First, he can attempt to appear credible himself, so that the judgments he makes in his speaking will be believed. And second, he can use judgments that are quotations from individuals who are perceived as credible. Thus, in a speech advocating extensions of the Medicare Bill, the use of quotations from the President, from physicians, from hospital employees, and others interested in and appearing qualified to discuss the subject will bolster the argument.

Some people appear to believe that credibility is "bad." They would argue that ideas should stand or fall on their own merit and that one should not take into account the personal characteristics of the individual presenting the ideas. As an ethical position, this argument may well have merit for the perfect world, in which every auditor is a rational man. However, we do not live in such a world, and auditors do respond to and change attitudes on the basis of the credibility of speakers. The effective speech communicator will realize this and attempt to make use of source credibility.

Source credibility is one factor that ought to govern the selection of judgments to be used in proof situations. The personal characteristics of listeners are other factors in this selection. This means the general motivational characteristics of individuals, both general demographic characteristics and certain personality characteristics.

The title of this chapter links judgments with motivation and suggests that motivation becomes more important when judgments are concerned than when either observations or inferences are in question. The linkage is somewhat tenuous, and it depends on the way in which the term "motivation" is defined. Psychologists use the term variously, and some feel that it should be abandoned, because it has come "to mean all things to all people." Before deciding to discard the term when discussing communication, however, let us look at some of the models of motivation that have traditionally been used.

One model suggests that individuals continuously strive toward a more inclusive and stable organization of their own cognitive state. This model suggests that when he receives communications, the individual will take them all in and then try to reconcile conflicting messages. This model assumes that man is rational, that it is only necessary to give him the facts, and he will go to work in a completely sane, logical, rational fashion to "make sense" out of the world around him. It assumes that man has developed certain basic beliefs and assumptions. He examines any messages that come in against the background of these beliefs and assumptions and then either accepts or rejects any portion of a message in line with basic assumptions. The model further suggests that judgments are accepted **only** when they are in line with previously held beliefs. It assumes that judgments play a part in decision-making and attitude change only to the extent that they are supportive of observed sense data.

A second model of motivation, a reward-punishment paradigm, assumes that man does not distinguish among observations, inferences, and judgments, but reacts solely to his view of whether they are personally rewarding or threatening to him. In this model, the social system becomes extremely important in determining the ways in which man views information. When an individual listens to the expression of a judgment, he will tend to check reactions with others in his immediate social system, and only then will change or refuse to change attitudes depending on the perception of the remainder of the members of his group. Group norms become an important determiner for the communicator, because such norms indicate what will be seen as rewarding by the group and what will be seen as nonrewarding or even threatening. In such a reward-punishment model, man does not need to possess rationality, but merely the ability to react to rewarding and nonrewarding situations in a consistent fashion, i.e., the ability to learn. The communicator, operating under a reward-punishment model of motivation, would select judgments for presentation to an auditor on the basis of their rewarding nature to the auditor, and not necessarily because they fit logically into an argument.

A third model of motivation, a personality paradigm, suggests that man's central approach to attitude formation and change, and thus to the judgments he hears and makes, will be one that emphasizes maintenance of the individual's self-image and self-integrity. He will accept messages that support his own personality and will reject messages that disturb his personality structure. Rationality enters only accidentally into decisions under such a model. Messages may actually be punishing to the individual's best interests, but if they support his personality, they will be accepted. The model assumes that individuals maintain their egos at different strength levels. An individual who has firmly established the structure of his own personality system tends to reject any information that would harm the system, whereas an individual who has left "loopholes" in his personality structure will be willing to consider messages that may seem threatening to him.

These three models of motivation overlap to some extent. Experimental evidence is still insufficient to establish one of the models as clearly superior to the others. Some of the evidence that is available, however, would suggest that reception of judgmental information is partly dependent on an interaction between certain personality characteristics and the manner in which the materials are presented. For example, the model of man as a rational being suggests that materials that are cast in a rational form will be better received than materials that appeal only to authorities as the reason for changing attitudes. In a study by Wagman,[3] people were divided into two groups depending on whether they were inclined toward an authoritarian personality or a nonauthoritarian personality. Then the groups were given messages that appealed either to "facts and reasons based on scientific study," or to suggestions based on "statements attributed to power figures." The results of the study showed:

1. The rational materials were more effective with the nonauthoritarian subjects, whereas the statements from authorities were more effective with the authoritarian subjects.

2. Some of the authoritarian subjects showed greater prejudice after the message than before. They actually showed negative effects.

3. Some of the nonauthoritarian subjects reacted negatively to authoritarian messages that were designed to make them less liberal. They actually became more liberal than before.

This study illustrated some of the problems that the communicator faces in attempting to make use of judgments in his messages. Available evidence tends to show that the ways in which man behaves depend on a number of different factors, and that a single model of motivation is probably insufficient to account for all the differential effects that might be produced.

The models of motivation just presented may help the speech communicator to organize his own thinking about the relationships between the judgments he uses in his speeches and the reception of

[3]M. Wagman, "Attitude Change and Authoritarian Personality," **Journal of Psychology**, 40 (1955), 3–24.

those speeches by auditors. Even if none of the three models can be considered entirely adequate to explain motivation, some combination of the three may well provide an adequate model for the communicator. Each of the three models assumes that certain characteristics that the individual possesses or develops through learning either facilitate or hinder the persuasive power of any message. It is possible to integrate relevant portions of the three models of motivation by examining the relationship between certain personal and social variables found in auditors and general persuasibility. The examination would suggest that individual traits are positively related to general persuasibility. That is, if an individual possesses Trait X, and research shows that Trait X is positively related to persuasibility, the communicator should find it easier to get acceptance of his message from the individual possessing Trait X than from the individual who does not possess Trait X. A number of such relationships have been studied. It is impossible to assert that the relationship exists just because a single study says that it does, but the relationships suggested below, both positive and negative, represent the best conclusions possible at this time:

1. There seems to be a positive relationship between persuasibility and low self-esteem. The individual who possesses feelings of anxiety or feelings of inadequacy seems to be somewhat more persuasible than the one who does not have such low self-esteem.[4]

2. There is some support for suggesting that individuals who are overly aggressive or hostile in their interpersonal relations are less persuasible than those who are not so aggressive or hostile.[5] Furthermore, some additional information tends to show that with teen-agers and even younger children, hostility and low persuasibility are related in boys, but the relationship doesn't seem to hold with girls.[6]

3. There is some support for a hypothesis that individuals who reflect an authoritarian personality pattern are more persuasible than those tending toward nonauthoritarian patterns.[7] This finding, however, has to be considered against those of the Wagman study, reported above, which does not disagree with this general finding

[4]Irving L. Janis and Peter B. Field, "Sex Differences and Personality Factors Related to Persuasibility," in **Personality and Persuasibility,** eds. Carl I. Hovland and Irving L. Janis (New Haven: Yale University Press, 1959), pp. 55–68.
[5]**Ibid.**
[6]**Ibid.**
[7]Harriett Linton and Elaine Graham, "Personality Correlates of Persuasibility," in **Personality and Persuasibility,** pp. 69–101.

but suggests that there may be an interaction between the type of message and authoritarianness.[8]

4. A number of studies have investigated the relationship between general persuasibility and intelligence. In general, they tend to show that when the groups are matched for educational level, no significant relationships can be found between persuasibility and intelligence.[9] It should be noted, however, that it is not suggested that no relationship exists between amount of education and persuasibility. There does seem to be a negative correlation between amount of education and general persuasibility, but intelligence is not defined in terms of educational level in these studies.

5. There is a considerable amount of research evidence to show that females are generally more persuasible than males. In most of the studies, the differences between men and women in terms of persuasibility are very small, but they are statistically significant and tend to show in a number of different studies.[10] Whether the relationship is an actual sex difference, or whether it occurs because of some educational differences, or because of some personality trait that is more prevalent in women than in men, is not yet determined.

These relationships provide some aid, at least, to the communicator in his task of predicting how auditors will respond to the materials he presents. Certainly, present research has not been able to provide all the information one would like to have about audiences. Future research should help with the problem of predicting. For the time being, however, the communicator must be able to utilize information drawn from the models already described, combining it with what persuasibility research has been able to provide in order to make estimates about the ways in which auditors will react.

The presentation of judgments

The next chapter will be concerned with some of the ways in which messages can be presented so as to obtain belief from auditors. However, a number of problems intimately connected with the presentation of judgments deserve consideration with the previous sections' general discussion of the role of judgments in obtaining be-

[8]Wagman, "Attitude Change and Authoritarian Personality."
[9]**Personality and Persuasibility**, pp. 237–238.
[10]Ibid., pp. 238–240.

lief. In particular, let us look closely at the special cases of intensity of appeal and the use of fear appeals.

Judgments emphasize values, and a judgment is a statement that places a value on some object, event, or contemplated activity. Values range along a continuum, however, and the speech communicator can choose the intensity of value he places on the object with which he is concerned. Below are three judgments varying in intensity of appeal to the auditor:

1. The proposal to require people on relief to give up their television sets is the most reprehensible suggestion ever to come from the Council Room.

2. The proposal to require people on relief to give up their television sets represents poor judgment on the part of the City Council.

3. The proposal to require people on relief to give up their television sets needs further clarification and elaboration before the City Council is able to evaluate the proposal.

These three judgments range from intense to slight in the appeal they make to any auditor. Is it possible to say that the more intense the appeal is, the more persuasive it will be?

Little experimental evidence is available in this area, but at least one study would suggest that the answer lies in an interaction between the auditor's original belief and the intensity of the appeal. An individual who was already generally negative toward the City Council, and already felt that most of its activities were poorly carried out, would probably respond favorably to Judgment 1. It fits with the expectations he already has about the Council. On the other hand, an individual who is favorably inclined toward the Council, and tends to believe that its activities are usually well done, is probably not going to accept the extreme statement represented by Judgment 1. Such an individual might refuse to change his attitude on the grounds that "this is what the opposition always says." On the other hand, a strong opponent of the Council will certainly be willing to agree with Judgment 3, and the chances are that Judgment 3, which seems to represent a more rational, reasoned approach (whether it is or not), has more chance of being accepted by proponents of the Council. This would tend to suggest that the speaker is always better off with judgments that are phrased in a less extreme manner.

Some research suggests that auditors may not know a logical

argument when they hear one, but that they do like the appearance of logicality in the arguments presented to them.[11] If this is true, then it is probably also true that the same individuals will appreciate a "reasonable approach" in the stating of a judgment. This is the best conclusion that can be made about the intensity of appeal used in a judgment. It needs to be modified, however, for one specific case. When the speaker wishes to intensify belief in an audience that is already committed to the position taken by the speaker, the extreme statement will serve this function. In our national political conventions, television reports speech after speech, all loaded with extreme statements about the wonders of one party and the treacheries of the other. The viewer may well wonder about the advisability of the "reasonable approach" when viewing such a convention. But here the audience is already committed to support of the party, and the party leaders are merely attempting to intensify belief in the candidates selected and the platform presented.

In making the extreme statement in the convention situation, the party leaders run little risk. They know that they could not attract members of the opposition party even if they were to use the reasonable approach, and they are more interested in raising the emotions of the party faithful to the heights required by a tough campaign than they are in attracting support from neutrals. Such use of intense statement, however, does not necessarily imply successful use of the statement in changing audience attitudes. Rather, the situation is such that the audience already has beliefs that are consistent with the position taken in the extreme judgment, and the judgment serves merely to reinforce or intensify the previous belief position. Thus, a conclusion about the use of intense or extreme judgments in proof situations has to be made in terms of the kind of audience being addressed. Given an audience with strong beliefs, the extreme statement can be used to reinforce or strengthen the position. Given an audience without strong beliefs, the extreme statement may serve only to alienate audience members.

Fear appeals present another problem in motivational proof. Suppose that a communicator wants to reduce accidents on American highways. He certainly can present statistics and other types of observations and inferences to show that certain safety measures will help to reduce accidents. But he can also present a series of

[11] Erwin P. Bettinghaus, unpublished study.

judgments regarding the consequences of disregarding such safety measures. He can make references to the personal disfigurement caused by many accidents. He can make predictions that individuals sitting in the room will be involved in an accident. Not only can he use judgments as proof materials, he can vary the strength of the fear appeals that he uses. But are such fear appeals effective in inducing belief?

A number of studies have been completed in this area. An early study by Janis and Feshbach examined the effect of strong, minimal, and intermediate fear appeals in messages designed to get high-school students to brush their teeth. The strong fear-appeal messages pointed to the number of cavities that would occur and drew eloquent word pictures of the results of not brushing. The intermediate and minimal fear-appeal messages became progressively more "rational" in their presentation. The results showed that what Janis and Feshbach called the minimal fear appeal was the most effective form of the communication ". . . in that it elicited (a) more resistance to subsequent counterpropaganda and (b) a higher incidence of verbal adherence, and perhaps a greater degree of behavioral conformity, to a set of recommended practices."[12] They found that the strong appeal was the most effective form in arousing interest and in raising emotional tension. But the strong form was not the form that seemed to result in ultimate changes in attitude.

A more recent study by Hewgill and Miller[13] casts some doubt on the generality of the findings in the Janis and Feshbach study. The study showed that the nature of the threat made in the message was the most important element in deciding the effectiveness of the message. The topic Hewgill and Miller was concerned about was civil defense. Mesages were constructed appealing to listeners to take certain civil-defense measures. Some forms of the message made strong fear appeals, suggesting that failure to take the measures would result in disaster for the individual or the country. Others suggested that disaster would result for the listener's family. The findings showed that minimal fear appeals were better than strong appeals, except when an appeal was made with respect to the auditor's family. A strong fear appeal, in which the health or safety

[12]Irving L. Janis and Seymour Feshbach, "Effects of Fear-Arousing Communications," **Journal of Abnormal and Social Psychology,** 48 (1953), 78–92.
[13]Murray A. Hewgill and Gerald R. Miller, "Source Credibility and Response to Fear-Arousing Communications," **Speech Monographs,** 32 (1965), 95–101.

of the listener's family was threatened, proved to be the most effective.

Obviously, more research is needed on this topic. A conclusion from the studies to date might be that fear appeals are effective when the object of the appeal is highly valued. When the appeal is made toward individuals or objects that are not so highly valued, more rational appeals will be more effective.

An appeal to fear is only one area that could be studied. The speech communicator can make appeals to other drives, such as hunger, thirst, patriotism, gregariousness, and the like. These areas have not been carefully studied, and suggestions for presentation cannot be made, but the communicator should recognize that appeals to other motives are certainly possible and should be considered in making decisions in speech construction.

Summary

This chapter has suggested that judgments are statements that place values on the objects and events of the world around us. To the extent that they are believed, they are treated and acted upon in exactly the same fashion as observations and inferences. Belief in judgments depends on the credibility of the communicator who presents the judgment, the characteristics of the auditor who listens to the judgment, and the appeal that the judgment makes.

SEVEN

Strategy and tactics in message preparation

When the speech communicator has collected and evaluated evidential materials on any topic, he must then make a decision about what position he will take regarding a conclusion. After his own conclusions have been made, he then faces the necessity of communicating his decisions to others. At this point in the communication process, a great many questions are likely to present themselves. Should the audience be given all the information that the speaker used to make his own decision? What if there are time limits on the amount of time he can use? Is there some best pattern that could be used to organize the speech? What does the nature of the audience tell the communicator about the materials he should be using? Some of these questions have been considered in other volumes in this series. Selection of materials, audience analysis, and general arrangement of materials, for example, are taken up specifically in other volumes. This chapter is concerned with some problems related to the arrangement of materials for proof situations, communication situations in which the intent of the speaker is to induce audience belief in a proposition or series of propositions.

The differences between various kinds of proof materials have already been discussed, and suggestions have been made regarding the use of proof materials in evaluating conclusions. This chapter will discuss a general model, the Toulmin model, helpful to the communicator in organizing his materials into formal argumentative units for presentation to an audience. The placement of materials within an argument, and within larger language units such as the formal speech, is covered in a separate section below. The chapter is directed toward oral-communication situations of a relatively formal nature, such as an appearance before the Kiwanis Club, a church group, the P.T.A., or the City Council. However, the materials to be dealt with are equally adaptable to more informal situations, such as group discussions, and so forth.

The Toulmin model

The average listener, and indeed the average communicator, has difficulty in recognizing a valid argument. Even when the material is in written form, as in an editorial, the reader will experience great difficulty in deciding whether the conclusions presented follow from the premises introduced. Yet written materials can be read and reread until the reader figures out whether the argument is to be believed. Under most circumstances, the auditor cannot relisten to the speech. He either is convinced the first time, or he rejects the argument. What the speech communicator needs is a method of organizing the materials he finds into a single pattern that will enable him to make decisions about those materials and to communicate the materials to a set of auditors.

Such a model or way of organizing an argument is proposed by the British philosopher Stephen Toulmin in his book **The Uses of Argument**.[1] Toulmin was disturbed by the difficulties of using the syllogism for detecting the validity of arguments. He was also disturbed because people did not seem to make their decisions according to the pattern set down by classical logic. So he proposed a new set of organizational patterns, designed to allow the communicator to organize his materials into a framework that will disclose the relationships between his propositions. Toulmin's basic ideas have been expanded for the formal debate situation by Douglas Ehninger and Wayne Brockriede in their book **Decision by Debate,** and by Russel

[1]Stephen Toulmin **The Uses of Argument** (Cambridge England: Cambridge University Press, 1958).

Figure 2. Simple Toulmin Model

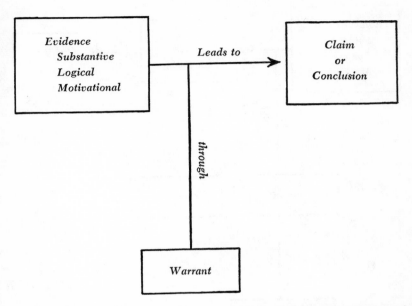

R. Windes and Arthur Hastings in **Argumentation and Advocacy.**[2] This chapter, however, presents the basic Toulmin organizational pattern adapted for communication situations in which the speaker wishes to induce belief in some proposed policy.

Toulmin suggests that all conclusions—all statements that express some policy based on the consideration of evidential materials —can be expressed as a series of propositions that relate the evidential materials to the conclusion. Some of the propositions represent actual data about the problem and some of them represent linking statements, statements that show the link between data statements and the conclusion statements. The model is shown in Figure 2. Note that there are three basic elements to any argument, the **evidence, warrant,** and **claim.** Figure 3 shows an expanded model capable of handling more complicated situations. It maintains the three elements of evidence, warrant, and claim, but adds the elements of **qualifier, reservation,** and **support for the warrant.** With these six elements, Toulmin claims to be able to

[2]Douglas Ehninger and Wayne Brockriede **Decision by Debate** (New York: Dodd, Mead & Company, Inc., 1963); Windes and Hastings, **Studies in Speech** (New York: Random House, Inc., 1965).

Figure 3. Modified Toulmin Model

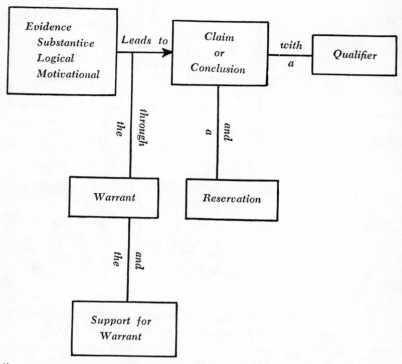

diagram any argument in such a fashion that the relationship between the parts of the argument become clear. Let us take up the six elements and define them in detail.

In its broadest sense, **evidence** is any data that can be used to establish a conclusion. Statements of fact, inferential statements, and judgmental statements can all serve as evidence. In the Toulmin organizational pattern, evidence is used as the basis from which conclusions can be drawn. A unit of evidence may consist of a single proposition representing an observation made by a single person, or it may be composed of a series of observations. Evidence may take the form of statistical materials, case histories, judgments made by some authority, or any other statements from which people might be inclined to reason.

As Toulmin used the term, the **claim** was any conclusion that followed from the evidence. This volume limits the claim to the proposition in which the communicator wishes to induce belief. Thus the claim may be a statement of fact, or an inference, or even a judgmental statement. The speaker who says, "Unemployment is increasing in the United States, and the government ought to do something about it," is moving from an evidential statement to a conclusion, or claim. The speaker wishes the audience to believe that the government ought to take certain actions. The claim may appear in the argument as simply as indicated in this brief example, or it might take the form of an entire series of policy propositions. A good example of the complicated claim is represented by the late President John F. Kennedy's speech to the nation after the Cuban missile crisis. He reviewed the evidence that the United States had collected and then made a series of statements representing what our policy would be as a result of examining the evidence. The claim was complex and required many statements.

The **warrant** is the statement that shows the reasoning that must have gone on between finding the evidence and making the claim. It may show the assumptions on which the claim is based or the method by which the evidence was evaluated. It is a "because," or a "why," or a "since" kind of statement. For example, the speaker might argue "Unemployment is increasing in the United States, and the federal government ought to do something about it, since the state governments obviously have not been able to cope with the problem." Here, the last part of the argument is the warrant and indicates the reason why the speaker makes his claim. In another example, the warrant might appear between the evidence and the claim: "Juvenile delinquency is increasing in our big cities, and since delinquency is closely related to crowded housing, the federal government ought to provide housing subsidies for families with low incomes and small children." Here, the warrant ties the claim to the evidence by making an assumption that delinquency and crowded housing are related. In still another example, the nature of the communicator's belief system is shown by the warrant, "Children today are getting physically soft, and Dodge High School ought to institute a compulsory physical-education program, since President Johnson says that if the nation is to be strong, we must have citizens that are physically fit." The argument is from an authority and indicates the underlying assumptions on which the speaker bases his conclusion.

These are the three basic elements of any argument. It may be that in the speech itself, the speaker will present only the evidence and his claim; but the warrant is implied, and the speaker may feel that showing the reasoning he used will be more likely to induce belief in the conclusion. In more complicated arguments, other statements are likely to be found, and these help the communicator decide on the believability of the claim made in the argument.

In the examples used in defining the warrant above, the reader might feel that the warrant provides an insufficient justification for the claim. When this situation arises, the warrant itself will need more support, in order to justify its use. Such backing is provided by the **support for the warrant.** These additional materials may be observations, or further opinions, or merely clarifying statements for the warrant. The one example used above could add support for the warrant by arguing: "Unemployment is increasing in the United States, and the federal government ought to do something about it, since the state governments obviously have not been able to cope with the problem, and our system of government provides for federal action when the states cannot act." In an expansion of another argument, the support for the warrant takes the form of an inference from history: "Negro citizens are segregated into ghetto areas in the United States, therefore the United States needs a fair housing law, since every citizen ought to be treated equally, and history shows that nations that do not provide for equal treatment cannot grow either economically or morally." The last part of the argument is the support for the warrant. What was true for the warrant is also true for the support for the warrant. One must distinguish between use of the support for the warrant in decision-making and in speech-making. The communicator may well choose not to present all of the statements in any argument to his auditors, although he uses the statements in deciding what claim he will advance.

In many policy areas, a claim may have to be limited in some way. It could be that a claim will apply if certain conditions are met, but not in other circumstances. It could be that a claim applies only in a certain area, or for certain people, or for a certain time of the year. The **reservation** sets forward the nature of any limitations that the communicator wishes to place on the claim he makes.

Below are two arguments. The first does not make use of a reservation, but the second does. Note that the second argument seems much easier to believe in than the first.

1. The underdeveloped nations of the world have a more rapidly rising birthrate than the developed nations. (**evidence**)

The United States should provide these nations with birth control information that will let them control their population. (**claim**)

We must take this action because we have a moral obligation to help underdeveloped nations. (**warrant**)

2. The underdeveloped nations of the world have a more rapidly rising birthrate than the developed nations. (**evidence**)

States should not provide information to nations whose religious and moral principles would outlaw control of births. (**reservation**)

We must take this action because we have a moral obligation to help underdeveloped nations. (**warrant**)

In the example cited, the reservation not only limits the claim made, but even seems to provide additional persuasive support for the claim. The reservation could be made even if there were no such countries as those suggested in the reservation. Most claims made in policy areas cannot be made without some limitations, because there will always be a hierarchy of policies that could be adopted. Reservations can specify the amount of money that can be used, or the future situation that might make the claim unworkable, or the limitations that might be placed on the claim from other policy decisions.

The **qualifier** is usually an adjective placed within the statement that forms the claim. To use an old example, take the claim that "Socrates was mortal." If one placed a qualifier within that claim, he might have "Socrates was probably mortal." The qualifier can be a term like "maybe," "mostly," "possibly" or "seldom." It can also be a phrase like "most of the time," "75 per cent of the cases," "in fewer than ten," or "only in rare circumstances." The qualifier is important to the communicator in making his decision regarding some claim. A claim that might not be acceptable without qualification could become acceptable with the proper qualifier added to the claim. The qualifier is also important in communicating a decision to an audience. People tend to suspect claims that "say too much" or "promise the world." The proper qualifier added to a claim may well let an auditor accept a claim that he would otherwise reject.

These six elements are sufficient to analyze any argument, even extremely complex arguments. As indicated, they may also serve the communicator as the organizing pattern for composing the materials that he will deliver to an audience. The Toulmin pattern does not claim to be logical in the same way that a syllogism is logical, but Toulmin suggests that it comes closer to the ways in which people ordinarily think about policy problems than do other patterns of analysis.

In the presentation thus far, this text has made use of very simple arrangements of the six elements. It is possible, however, to use the six elements to analyze arguments of considerable complexity. More than one piece of evidence may be used, and more than one claim advanced from the evidence. There may be several warrants underlying the claim made, with several kinds of support for each warrant. It is quite possible that the claim or claims made will need to have several reservations applied to them and that each claim will have to be qualified in some way. Below is presented an argument, identified in terms of the parts of the argument, which shows some of the complexity and versatility of the model.

More than half the world's population goes to bed hungry at night. **(evidence)**

The world has more than doubled its population in the last thirty years. **(evidence)**

Present figures show that the world will again double its population to approximately six billion by the year 2000. **(evidence)**

With present agricultural methods, the world cannot sustain even a minimum health standard with six billion people, says Dr. X of the World Health Organization. **(evidence)**

We must institute a program of world population control within the next few years. **(claim)**

Such a program should probably **(qualifier)** be administered by the United Nations, **(claim)** since only the United Nations can be said to truly represent the entire world. **(warrant)**

Unless nations move within the next few years to institute their own

Figure 4. Toulmin Model and General Patterns of Proof

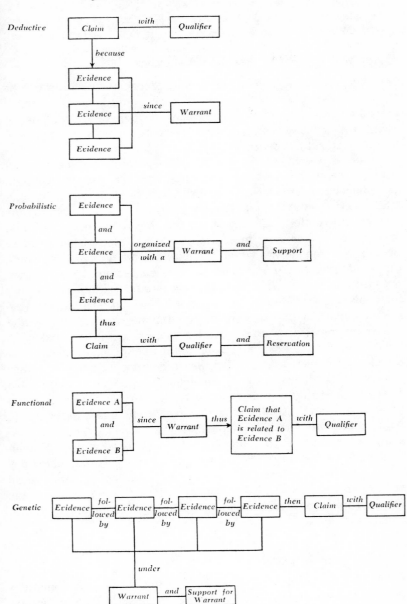

programs, or unless a general world war begins, **(reservations)** the United Nations, which Secretary General Dag Hammarskjöld once said was the one remaining hope of civilization, **(support for warrant)** must seek the cooperation of the world in making life on this globe possible for mankind. **(restatement of claim)**

This is a complex argument, yet all the propositions within it can be analyzed by use of the Toulmin approach. Furthermore, although the argument has been stripped of many of its rhetorical qualities, it would, with a little polish, make a perfectly appropriate argument for use in an actual speech.

Earlier, it was suggested that the four general patterns of proof were the deductive, probabilistic, functional, and genetic. A classical syllogistic approach is used easily only with the deductive pattern. However, the Toulmin elements can be used with any of the four general patterns already discussed. Figure 4 shows potential arrangements of some of the basic elements, if one wishes to apply the model to the general situation. Note that the type of information that would go into any one of the patterns suggested in Figure 3 has not been specified. The communicator would not expect to use materials fitting a functional explanation within the pattern suggested for a genetic explanation. The Toulmin model is an aid to the communicator in organizing his materials prior to making a decision and before communicating the results of his decision to an audience. The model does **not,** however, give the communicator any rules to follow in evaluating an argument that has been constructed to any of the patterns already suggested. In part, no set of rules can be devised that will allow a communicator to make decisions in policy areas with the kind of precision that he might desire. However, two steps are possible. First, the elements of the Toulmin model can be examined, and suggestions can be made regarding any effect omissions or errors in constructing a pattern might have on some of the conclusions that can be drawn. Second, some of the common mistakes people make in reasoning, i.e., **fallacies,** can be considered.

Mistakes in proof patterns

A "mistake" in proof, for the purposes of this discussion, comprises any error in argument construction that is likely to lead an auditor to refuse to believe the conclusion **because of the error.** Formal validity is not the primary consideration, rather it is the nature of belief patterns in auditors. Such mistakes can be made in the construction of any of the six elements.

The most frequent mistake in introducing **evidence** is the failure to use enough evidence for the claim made. Seldom is a broad claim supportable by a single piece of evidence or a single quotation. It is too easy to find counterevidence in most policy areas, and unless the communicator has presented enough evidence to overcome the possible weight of any counterevidence, he is not likely to be believed. It is extremely difficult to answer the question, "How much evidence is enough?" Perhaps the best rule that can be followed is to suggest that the communicator examine the evidence he has, and attempt to determine whether it is (a) convincing to himself; and (b) at least sufficient to counter any of the pieces of opposing evidence that might exist.

A second mistake that is frequently made in the presentation of evidence is a failure to use evidence that is related to the claim made. For example, the United States recently cut off the program by which Mexican migrant labor was imported every year to aid in harvesting American crops. In 1965 cherry growers in Michigan refused to harvest much of the crop, letting it rot on the trees. It could be argued that the failure to allow Mexican pickers into the United States resulted in the cherry crop's being allowed to rot. The growers took their action, however, because of the low price offered for their cherries, and the low price was the result of bumper crops in previous years. To argue that the evidence regarding the policy on migrant labor was the result of cherries rotting on the trees would be a failure to use evidence actually related to the claim made.

The most frequent mistake made in using the **warrant** is to base a claim on a warrant that is insufficient to justify the claim in the eyes of the audience. For example, the communicator may believe that any statement by the President is sufficient to justify a claim made. An audience is not likely to take such a view, and would reject the claim made, if the warrant is of such a nature.

A second error lies in using superstition as a warrant. To claim that some policy will now be necessary because an individual failed to throw salt over his left shoulder, or because a mirror was broken, is obviously to use a warrant that cannot relate evidence to claim.

Faulty **claims,** as has already been mentioned, frequently result when more is claimed than the evidence can justify. President Kennedy would not have been justified in arguing from a single eyewitness report smuggled out of Cuba that a threat to the United States actually existed. He might have been justified in concluding from such an eyewitness account that the country should attempt to obtain aerial photos of missile sites. In the first case, the evidence cited was related to the claim, but there was not enough of it. In the second, the evidence is the same, but the claim is more believable.

Mistakes in **qualifiers** are difficult to detect. They generally result from using a qualifying word or phrase that is so strong that it cannot be accepted. To say that the population explosion is an important world problem is a claim that seems believable when sufficient evidence is presented. To suggest that the population explosion is "the most" important problem might be hard to get people to believe. Such a qualifier might not win acceptance.

Too often, the error made with the **reservation** is to ignore it. Yet few claims can be made without considering other possible changes in policy, or other potential moves, that might alter the claim made. Another mistake is to make too many reservations, so many that the applicability of the claim to anything in the real world is hard to see. This is the result of an overabundance of "ifs." The speaker may say, "If this happens, and if that happens, and if this should come to pass, then X will happen." He may be making an accurate conclusion, but it is likely that he will not receive the attention that his claim deserves, because of the many limitations that he has placed on the claim.

The same mistakes that are made in using evidence can be made with the **support for a warrant.** The communicator may fail to use sufficient support to justify the warrant made, or he may use support that is not related to the warrant. Either one may result in rejection of the warrant, and thus in audience disbelief concerning the relationship between evidence and claim.

Any of the reasons cited in this brief analysis of some of the mistakes that can be made might result in rejection by an auditor of the claim made. It must also be pointed out, however, that rejection can occur even if the argument **is** well constructed. Belief depends far more on the predispositions of the auditor than it does on the manner in which an argument is constructed. However, the manner in which the communicator constructs his messages may result in acceptance by an individual who has not determined his own position, or who has not considered the matter before.

Fallacies

A **fallacy** can be defined as a mistake in reasoning, a mistake that allows an individual to consider evidence and to draw a claim from it that is not justified. The study of fallacies is very old, dating back as far as Aristotle. Some of the mistakes noted in the last section can be classified as fallacies, but some other common fallacies will be discussed here. The communicator is warned against fallacies for two reasons. First, fallacies lead individuals to make decisions that are not justified by the materials presented. And second, many of the common fallacies are recognizable by audiences and will result in rejection of any claim advanced by the communicator.

The classical fallacy is the one sometimes labeled **"post hoc, ergo propter hoc** [after this, therefore because of this]." This is the error of assuming that merely because an event follows another in time, the earlier caused the later. In its ridiculous form, one might argue that because I broke a mirror yesterday, I fell and sprained my ankle today. The assumption in most superstitions, old wives' tales, and magic is a **post hoc** assumption. It argues that because one thing happened, another must be tied to it. But merely following in time is not **sufficient** grounds to argue cause, although it is a **necessary** ground.

Faulty causal reasoning probably accounts for more mistakes in proof situations than any other single fallacy. It is important to establish cause in many policy areas, and it seems so plausible to argue that the appearance of one new phenomenon is the cause of another. After World War II, for example, many people argued that any rainstorm, any flood, any natural disaster must have been caused by the dropping of atomic bombs. Indeed, many people still believe that weather is largely influenced by atomic testing, in spite of the complete lack of scientific support of such a theory. But it seems so believable that it has received support even from educated individuals. Timing alone, however, can never be used to account for causality.

One of the most common arguments in favor of the Medicare

Bill that was passed in the United States in 1965 was that a similar program works in England and, therefore, that it should work in the United States. This is evidence, with a claim that it will work here. The warrant is unstated, but it must be a belief that the United States and England can be compared with respect to medical care. The argument is an argument from analogy, reasoning from what happened in one situation to what might happen in another situation. Let us suppose that two people are both members of the same church—they share the quality of church membership. Reasoning from analogy would argue that because the people share church membership, and because one individual is a poor credit risk, that the other must also be a poor credit risk.

At some point, every analogy must break down, because there will always be some place where two objects or two events differ in nature or degree. However, if there are many points of similarity between two events, it is possible to generalize from the results of one event to the probable results of another. **Faulty analogy** results when two events, or objects, or people are not alike in the characteristics that are being compared, or in characteristics relevant to those being compared.

A special case of faulty analogy is sometimes called the **fallacy of composition.** It is the assumption that what is true of individuals alone will be true of individuals in a group situation. It is the warrant that says that the whole is equal to the sum of its parts. This may be true, but it is likely that people will behave differently in groups than they behave separately. A recent example of the fallacy of composition is to be found in the argument that price supports help the cotton farmer, the wheat farmer, and the soybean farmer, therefore, price supports for all commodities would help all farmers. Maybe this is the case, but the analogy between cotton, wheat, and soybeans does not necessarily hold true for beef, pork, and chicken.

The dilemma results when two or more claims seem justified from the evidence presented. Some dilemmas are real. The individual who is asked to choose to have an operation that could result in death on the operating table, or choose not to have the operation and run the risk of dying of cancer may face a real dilemma. The **faulty dilemma** results when one of the claims is specious, when the evidence really does not justify making the claim. A faulty dilemma can also result when there is a third alternative possible, but never stated. For example, take the case of a farmer who is raising wheat for sale. It could be argued that such a farmer can never get ahead; when he produces an excellent crop, the price falls, and when the price is up, his crop will probably be poor. Either way, the argument goes, the farmer never wins. This is a faulty dilemma, because it fails to consider the possibilities of government price supports as aids to the farmer. It also makes the assumption that when one farmer has a good crop, all other farmers will also have good crops.

Any dilemma may be examined in two ways. Either one can question whether all possible claims have been mentioned, that is, whether all alternatives have been exhausted; or one can question whether the claims suggested have the same merit. The communicator can frequently then "make sense" out of what appears to be a hopeless situation.

This fallacy, and several to follow, are **psychological fallacies.** They tend to prevent decisions from being made on the merits of the case, and instead suggest that they be made on the basis of the emotions stirred up by the language used. The use of **emotional language** in argument construction may assist in obtaining belief. But it may, equally, prevent belief and it is likely to do so when the auditor has been relatively neutral or mildly opposed to the claim advanced. Emotive language capable of such effects might occur in phrases such as "There are always a few malcontents to oppose real progress," "The Governor is always ready to support legislation that will lead to increased freedom," "We are engaged only in peaceful propaganda," "This action denotes a deliberate plot against the company," and "The speaker harangued the audience."

It is certainly possible to use words to arouse vivid imagery, but such use may obscure the specific action that is being advocated. The communicator must be sure that the audience he is addressing will be inclined to agree with him or run the risk of having the argument rejected for irrelevant reasons.

Special pleading is the fallacy of presenting only materials that tend to support the claim one wishes to present, when other evidence is clearly present. For example, the Surgeon General of the United States released a report that tended to show a relationship between smoking and lung cancer. Other research organizations came forward to argue that their research had not shown the kind of relationships shown in the Surgeon General's report. However, their research had been supported by the large tobacco companies. It certainly could be that research scientists would disagree on so complicated a subject, but the arguments from the research organizations supported by the tobacco companies become suspect. They seem to be a case of special pleading. In other situations, special pleading occurs when an individual argues differently from the same set of materials. A "good buy" for me is a "steal" for you. What is aggression for one country becomes preventive war for another. These are all cases of special pleading.

When a communicator has a position that cannot be adequately supported, he may attempt to draw attention away from it by directing attention to some side issue. This is considered drawing a **red herring,** a false trail, over the real issue. In court, a lawyer with a weak case may attempt to cloud the issue by introducing many character witnesses to show that his client attends church regularly and gives money freely to charity. This tends to obscure the fact that the individual may have obtained the money he donated by embezzlement.

Another way of introducing the red herring is to throw out so much evidence that the really relevant materials are obscured. The communicator is giving all the evidence, but he introduces evidence that is not material to the case, and embeds the important materials in a sea of trivia. The auditor finds it impossible to separate relevant from the irrelevant.

There are other fallacies that could be considered in this section, but most of them have been discussed in other sections within the book. The logical fallacies have been covered in Chapter 5, and many of the psychological fallacies, in Chapter 6. It remains to point out that fallacious arrangement of materials makes it difficult for the communicator to arrive at a considered decision regarding some area of policy. Many of the fallacies are extremely persuasive argumentative structures, and they may well result in changes in audience beliefs. For those who have been trained to detect fallacies, however, the argument will carry little weight. For those wishing to see clearly the relationships between evidence and claim, the fallacy is disturbing and unconvincing.

Placement of materials

This section will consider two problems in tactics: Where does the communicator place his important materials within the message? What differences result from messages that the communicator has garbled in some way? It is not concerned with the effects of argument importance or garbling messages on the amount of learning that seems to occur, except as learning is related to changes in belief. In neither of these two areas of concern has sufficient research been completed to make possible any final recommendations. But the research available is provocative and deserves consideration.

Let us assume that I have examined some evidence and have arrived at a general policy decision that I would like to communicate to others. The chances are that some of the material I have will be more important than other material, in terms of relating it to the claims I am making, and in terms of the impact I expect it to have on an auditor. Where do I place the information within my speech? Should I put it first, where it will "hit" the auditor immediately? Should it go in the center of the speech, after I have been able to interest the auditor in the material? Or should it be the last thing I tell him, so that it will be fresh in his mind?

There are a number of studies and reports concerning the effect of order.[3] The most general conclusion that can safely be drawn from these studies is that placing the most important issue either first or last is preferable to placing it in the middle. No study shows a preference for a pyramidal arrangement. However, the studies are fairly well split between those that tend to show a preference for first placement and those that tend to show a preference for last placement. None of the findings shows marked preference for either first or last position. However, a study by McGuire[4] suggests that placing materials that seem to appeal to the needs of the audience first, then following with somewhat less desirable materials, will produce more effect. Studies by Cohen[5] tend to support the McGuire findings.

Many other factors are more important than the order in which materials are placed. The commitment of the auditor, the number and nature of preceding speeches, the nature of the subject to be

[3]See specifically Carl I. Hovland, **et al., The Order of Presentation in Persuasion** (New Haven: Yale University Press, 1957).
[4]**Ibid.,** p. 136.
[5]**Ibid.,** pp. 135, 136.

discussed undoubtedly all play a part in the way in which materials will be received. When the task of the communicator is first to obtain the attention of the auditor to the subject, and then to interest him in the materials, perhaps the best conclusion is that the strongest materials should be placed first within the total speech.

The other problem under discussion is much clearer. Imagine that as a speaker I am relatively careless in my use of grammar. I mix up my words at times and make many mistakes. What effect will it have on the perception of my audience? There are two studies in this area, one dealing with the effects of grammatical error on comprehension and opinion change, and one dealing with the effects of switching statements out of normal order.

The first study is by Sencer,[6] who looked at the effects of grammatical error. He produced a series of messages and varied the number of grammatical errors within them. The same materials were in each message, but some messages had many more than the normal number of tense errors, gender errors, misspellings, and so forth. The results are interesting. They showed that the readers of the messages had little trouble in understanding the content of the message, but that they resented having to read messages with a great number of grammatical errors. There was significantly less opinion change when the messages had a great number of grammatical errors than when they had few errors.

The second study was by Darnell,[7] who produced a message with fifteen statements arranged in a logical order, with a claim at the beginning, and supporting materials neatly arranged below the claim. Then he systematically varied the order of presentation by switching statements around in the messages until he had seven messages, ranging from one in perfect order to one with a maximum amount of garbling. Again, there were few differences in learning. But there were highly significant differences in opinion change in favor of the messages that were in relatively logical order.

Apparently, what is operating is a set of expectations about messages. The auditor expects messages to be free of error, and when

[6]Robert A. Sencer, "An Investigation of the Effects of Incorrect Grammar on Attitude and Comprehension in Written English Messages," unpublished doctoral dissertation, Michigan State University, 1965.
[7]Donald Darnell, "The Relation Between Sentence Order and the Comprehension of Written English," **Speech Monographs,** 30 (1963), 97–100.

they are not, he resents it, and takes out this resentment by refusing to believe what is being claimed, even though he may arrive at perfect understanding. Similar results were discovered in a study regarding delivery. Good delivery was preferred to poor and resulted in more opinion change, even though, in both cases, the speaker was the same and the message was the same.[8] Auditors expect certain types of messages, and persuasion goes down when the communicator fails to meet those expectations.

Summary

This chapter has discussed the presentation of materials relating to a communicator's policy decisions. The Toulmin model was suggested as a device for organizing materials prior to making decisions about the collected evidence. A basic model, depending on the relationships between evidence, warrants, and claims, and a more complex model, adding reservations, qualifiers, and support for the warrants, were considered.

The chapter also considered a number of fallacies in reasoning, suggesting that such fallacies make it impossible for the communicator to arrive at conclusions that adequately represent his evidence. It also suggested that the use of fallacies, although possibly persuasive to some audience members, will not be persuasive to many others, and should be avoided. Finally, it discussed some problems in strategy and tactics concerned with the placement of materials.

[8]Erwin P. Bettinghaus, "The Operation of Congruity in an Oral Communication Situation," unpublished portions of doctoral dissertation, University of Illinois, 1959.

Selected bibliography

Berelson, Bernard, and Steiner, Gary A. **Human Behavior: An Inventory of Scientific Findings.** New York: Harcourt, Brace & World, 1964.

Berlo, David K. **The Process of Communication.** New York: Holt, Rinehart and Winston, 1960.

Brown, Roger William. **Words and Things.** Glencoe: The Free Press, 1958.

Cherry, Colin. **On Human Communication: A Review, a Survey, and a Criticism.** Cambridge, Mass., and New York: The Technology Press of Massachusetts Institute of Technology and John Wiley & Sons, 1957.

Dewey, John. **Logic: The Theory of Inquiry.** New York: Henry Holt, 1938.

Ehninger, Douglas, and Brockriede, Wayne. **Decision by Debate.** New York: Dodd, Mead, 1963.

Festinger, Leon. **A Theory of Cognitive Dissonance.** Stanford: Stanford University Press, 1957.

Hall, Edward Twitchell. **The Silent Language.** Garden City: Doubleday, 1959.

Hovland, Carl I., and Janis, Irving L., eds. **Personality and Persuasibility.** New Haven: Yale University Press, 1959.

———, ———, and Kelley, Harold H. **Communication and Persuasion: Psychological Studies of Opinion Change.** New Haven: Yale University Press, 1953.

121

————, et al. **The Order of Presentation in Persuasion.** New Haven: Yale
University Press, 1957.

Lippman, Walter. **Public Opinion.** New York: Macmillan, 1922.

Minnick, Wayne C. **The Art of Persuasion.** Boston: Houghton Mifflin,
1957.

Rogers, Everett M. **Diffusion of Innovations.** New York: The Free Press
of Glencoe, 1962.

Rokeach, Milton. **The Open and Closed Mind: Investigations into the
Nature of Belief Systems and Personality Systems.** New York:
Basic Books, 1960.

Schramm, Wilbur Lang, ed. **The Process and Effects of Mass Communication.** Urbana: The University of Illinois Press, 1954.

Taylor, James Garden. **The Behavioral Basis of Perception.** New
Haven: Yale University Press, 1962.

Toulmin, Stephen. **The Uses of Argument.** Cambridge, England: Cambridge University Press, 1958.

Index

THE BOBBS-MERRILL SERIES IN *Speech Communication*

•